M000116996

COURAGE

POWERFUL LESSONS IN
LEADERSHIP, STRENGTH,
AND THE WILL TO SUCCEED

COURAGE

POWERFUL LESSONS IN LEADERSHIP, STRENGTH, AND THE WILL TO SUCCEED

JOHN SPERZEL

© 2021 by John Sperzel

All rights reserved. No part of this publication may be reproduced or transmitted in any form or by any means, electronic or mechanical, including photography, recording, or any information storage and retrieval system, without permission in writing from the author.

Requests for permission to make copies of any part of the work should be emailed to the following address: johnsperzel@gmail.com

Published and distributed by Merack Publishing

Library of Congress Control Number: 2021901912
Sperzel, John,
Courage: Powerful Lessons in Leadership, Strength and the Will to Succeed
Paperback: ISBN 978-1-949635-62-1
Hardcover: ISBN 978-1-949635-64-5
eBook: ISBN 978-1-949635-63-8

DEDICATION

This book is dedicated to Alex Coe,
who made the decision to be an organ donor,
and saved my life.

CONTENTS

INTRODUCTION

The word courage is defined as:

cour·age
/ˈkərij/
noun:

1. the ability to do something that frightens one.
   "she called on all her courage to face the ordeal."

2. strength in the face of pain or grief.
   "he fought his illness with great courage."

Wikipedia defines courage (also called bravery or valor) as "the choice and willingness to confront agony, pain, danger, uncertainty, or intimidation." It breaks the concept into two parts: physical courage and moral courage. **Physical courage** is bravery in the face of physical pain, hardship, even death or threat of death, while **moral courage** is the ability to act rightly in the face of popular opposition, shame, scandal, discouragement, or personal loss. The classical virtue of fortitude is also translated as "courage," but includes the aspects of perseverance and patience.

Can you see why I absolutely love the word and the concept of courage?

Just wait.

It gets even better!

The word itself is derived from the Middle English term *courage*, denoting the heart as the seat of feelings, which comes from the Old French word *corage*, stemming from the Latin word *cor* (heart). That's right: my favorite word, COURAGE, comes from the Latin word for HEART!

Origin

To top it all off, if you look up the word heart in the dictionary, you'll see the meaning of heart is synonymous with courage. The two go together and are inextricably linked—and that synergistic relationship forms the basis for the format of this book. In a style that could be described as "one part memoir, one part manual," the first half of this book is my story (the memoir). It's a tale of courage—both the physical and the moral courage described in the definition of the word itself.

But just like in life: it's not about what happens to you that's important… it's *who you choose to become as a result of what happens to you* that really matters. And that's part two (the manual). That's where we'll search deeper into my story to find the principles and the powerful lessons and the duplicatable system for success in life that you as the reader can follow, and repeat, to gain a predictable and measurable outcome, over and over again.

With time and reflection and testing, I've realized there are five key elements I feel are absolutely essential for success in life and business. To keep them simple and easy to remember, each element is a letter—a puzzle piece—which, when put together, is the H.E.A.R.T. acronym:

> H = Hard Work
> E = Excellence
> A = Attitude
> R = Resilience
> T = Teamwork

If these five elements are at the HEART of success, when you combine them with passion and your own personal strengths— your unique *genius*—you become truly unstoppable.

And *then*, if you pair those five elements and your passion and talents and skill set with your life story—your unique *experience*—that is where TRUE PURPOSE resides.

> **OUR LIFE STORY CAN OFTENTIMES REVEAL OUR TRUE PURPOSE IF WE HAVE THE COURAGE TO ALLOW IT TO EMERGE FROM THE ASHES OF ADVERSITY AND CONNECT THE DOTS OF OUR LIFE IN REVERSE.**

My own personal passion is developing and commercializing products and technologies that improve or save people's lives.

But what about my natural talents and unique genius?

From a very young age, I knew I wanted to be a CEO. I don't think I ever put an actual name to it until I was in my first leadership role, but I've always wanted more and more leadership responsibility. It wasn't a specific job in my mind—I was just thirsty for more, to lead more people and to lead more functions... it was always about wanting more breadth and depth in that capacity. And then, when I was a Vice President at a global healthcare company in my early thirties, I *saw* the job I had always wanted—CEO—and realized that what I had envisioned all my life actually had a name and a title.

I'm a laser-focused guy, so you might assume that once I knew what I was aiming for it all just happened immediately. Leadership at the highest level isn't something that happens overnight. It takes time—and, more importantly—*experience.* My career has definitely not been a straight line to advance from a sales representative, where I began, to the chief executive officer of a Nasdaq-listed public company, where I am today. That was truly by design.

Gaining experience and honing your skill set is a journey.

I worked as a vice president for ten years at a company that was pioneering glucose self-testing for people with diabetes. When it was acquired by Roche, I made the difficult decision to leave. It is never easy to leave a great company, especially one where you have been very successful, but I had a specific reason. To that point, my career *had* been very linear: sales, sales management, marketing, then bigger sales management, and even bigger sales management. While I felt that my skill set was much broader, my experience was actually very narrow. Though I had successfully risen through the ranks of sales and marketing, I had no operations experience at the time. Yes, I had depth in sales and marketing, but I didn't have any breadth. Think of it like the actress or actor who plays a similar role in their first five movies; people wonder, *can this person succeed playing different roles?* I knew I had to get operations experience at that point or it might be difficult to get later.

To get this experience, I joined Instrumentation Laboratory, a private healthcare company based in Massachusetts with a parent company based in Barcelona, Spain. The company had two business units, one focused on critical care testing and the other focused on coagulation testing. The products were intended for hospital intensive care units, operating rooms, and laboratories. I went in what some might view as a "sideways" direction, but the truth is: I got more operations experience in the next four years than I probably could have gotten anywhere else in twenty. I learned the inner workings of manufacturing operations and research and development, and I also added to my growing international experience.

I then went back to a large company, Bayer Diagnostics, as VP of worldwide marketing and business development. We developed and marketed world-leading products in diabetes, coagulation, urinalysis, and critical care testing. I also volunteered for a "project" to restructure, refocus, and improve the company's business in Japan. Bayer ended up being acquired by Siemens, but within a handful of years, I went from a person with little breadth, to one with significant commercial, operational, and international experience.

When Bayer was acquired by Siemens, I joined a London-based public company as the President of their US subsidiary. I was tasked with building an entire US organization from the ground up. It was a blank piece of paper to build a strategy, lease a building, hire a team, obtain regulatory approvals, and launch a product. It happened to be in a field that I knew very well—diabetes. For me, it was a chance to put the skills and experience I had gained over the last fifteen to twenty years to work. It felt like someone was saying to me, "OK, big shot. Let's see if you can actually do this." And it was wildly successful. Sales exploded. I was asked to join the board of directors of the American Diabetes Association New England Region, which increased our visibility. We won the vendor of the year award from the largest physician office distributor in the United States—ahead of Abbott, Roche, and many other leading companies. And we won it again the next year, something no company had ever done. The company was acquired in 2011, and is now part of Abbott Diagnostics.

And that led to my first role as CEO.

It was for a company that had just been acquired by one of the best private equity firms in the world—certainly one of the best in healthcare—Warburg Pincus. The company I inherited was hemorrhaging everywhere. I leaned on the turnaround business improvement skills I had developed with the Barcelona company, and then later refined with the project in Japan. We immediately turned the company around, and won an award for the most dramatic transformation amongst Warburg's portfolio companies. In a short amount of time, I was able to demonstrate I could lead a whole company as CEO and make the really tough decisions to improve a business. It was an incredible experience for me, and the company was ultimately sold to the Werfen Group (the Barcelona firm I mentioned earlier). Yes, it is indeed a small world.

And that led to my first role as the CEO of a public company—the pinnacle in business leadership—and the ultimate expression of my gifts and talents in a professional capacity.

I started out simply by following my passion (developing and commercializing products and technologies that improve or save people's lives), and I paired that with my strengths and unique genius (leadership). Over time, I gained, honed and built my skill set through experience (spending the first third of my career in diabetes testing, the middle third in critical care, and the balance in infectious diseases). At that point in my career—at the intersection of passion, talent, and experience—I truly felt unstoppable.

I was the CEO at Chembio Diagnostics for six years, where I had to go out and actually raise money—not just from a friendly parent company, or private equity firm with a checkbook, or the board that hired me—but from investors who didn't know me. I had to convince them to bet on me and my team, raise money, build a really strong strategy, and change a product pipeline. And we did a great job. In fact, we crushed it. We developed and commercialized rapid diagnostic tests to address some of the world's infectious disease threats like HIV, Zika, and Ebola.

As amazing as it was, there was so much more to come that would bring my personal and professional life into alignment beyond what I ever could have imagined—to take my job from that of a career to a *calling*. The building blocks I've just outlined, combined with my technical experience, led me to become a strong candidate for multiple public company CEO roles. But, when I decided to pursue a job I really wanted in order to make a difference—T2 Biosystems—it was that foundation *combined with my life story*, which you're about to read, that put me in a position where I became the natural, obvious choice for them and could live out my own TRUE PURPOSE here on earth.

I've spent a lot of time in hospitals around the world because of the jobs I've had as a sales rep, sales leader, business unit head, or a president and CEO, and I've spent an enormous amount of time with customers in those hospitals, working to save lives. Little did I know that the most important part of my career path was about to come full circle: spending time in hospitals around the world fighting for my *own* life, and becoming one of those customers myself.

PART ONE
MY STORY

CHAPTER 1

In 2017, I was serving as the CEO of a Nasdaq-listed public company, Chembio Diagnostics, doing exactly what I love to do—advancing life-saving technologies. I had literally been on a three-week international trip; I was in Malaysia to meet with the team from a company we had recently acquired, and Brazil and Mexico to meet with government officials. Then I flew back to the US, met with investors in San Francisco, and then went on to see my son, who was going to college in Nevada. After that whirlwind trip, I flew back to Boston only to hop on another flight—to Aruba—for a much-needed week of vacation with my girlfriend, Rhonda.

We arrived in Aruba on the afternoon of Easter Sunday, checked-in to the hotel, and decided to check out the property. As we walked out of the lobby toward the beach, we were greeted with the perfect weather that Aruba is known for; bright sunshine, temperatures in the high eighties, and a slight breeze. It's easy to see why Aruba carries the nickname *One Happy Island*. Our first day was pretty uneventful: we walked on the beach, exercised in the gym, had an early dinner, and went to sleep at about nine o'clock.

Less than twelve hours into our vacation, things took a sudden turn. Rhonda woke up at two or three in the morning, after hearing me make a strange noise. She put her hand on me as if to say, *honey, you're having a bad dream*, but I didn't move. She shook me but I still didn't wake up. I was soaked with sweat and completely unresponsive. She jumped out of bed, flipped on the light, and felt a wave of panic as she realized I was unconscious. Now, this is Aruba and there's no 911 to call, so she started shaking me and pounding on my chest. No response. Nothing. No sign of life. She ran downstairs to get help, and while she was gone, I miraculously woke up. I realized something was terribly wrong. I was alone in the room. My heart was racing. I was disoriented, lightheaded and nauseous. I instinctively got up from the bed and walked toward the bathroom. I heard Rhonda's voice as the door opened and said, "Rhonda, we need a doctor. Something's seriously wrong with me." She said, "I know, John, I thought you were dead. I'm here and I have help." She was standing in the doorway with the hotel security guard.

The security guard took me by the arm and walked me to the stairway, down two flights of stairs, and into the hotel lobby. When we arrived at the lobby, I was expecting an ambulance— but there was nothing. We walked outside and he said the driver would be here any minute. I still felt disoriented and lightheaded, so sat down on the curb and said to security, "Look, I need to get to a hospital *now*. Something is seriously wrong with me, and I don't know what it is." A few minutes later, a car pulled up. It's about three in the morning and I was expecting an ambulance but it's a taxi. The hotel security helps me into the back seat and instructs the driver to take me to the hospital. I asked the driver how long it would take to get to the hospital and he responded "six minutes." I said, "Please do it in three."

The driver pulled up to the hospital emergency room entrance and said, "We're here—just go in those doors." When I walked into the emergency room, the person in the ER said, "We need you to fill out some paperwork before you can be seen."

"We don't have time for paperwork." I said. "I need to see a doctor, now."

An emergency room doctor came out, saw my condition, checked my vitals, and recognized it wasn't good. My heart rate was out of control—it was probably close to 200 beats per minute. He said, "I'm sorry, this is going to be uncomfortable. I would normally sedate you, but we don't have time for that." He completed a medical procedure called cardioversion, where electrodes were placed on my chest and electric shocks were sent to my heart to restore a normal heart rhythm.

I spent most of the day in the emergency room at Horacio Oduber Hospital, the only hospital on the small island of Aruba. Sometime in the first couple of hours, the doctor said, "John, we need to get you to a hospital in the United States—one that has the resources to handle whatever is causing your heart complications. We're going to get a medical jet, but it has to come from the US. It'll take several hours to get here and then we're going to send you to a hospital in Miami, Florida." He was able to get me stabilized, and by early evening, the jet had arrived. I was transported to the airport—this time by a hospital ambulance—and I boarded the medical jet, headed to the US. The nice thing about leaving a Caribbean island in the middle of the night on a medical jet is there is no requirement to go through customs; my passport was literally stamped as I boarded the plane. The plane, operated by JET ICU, was outfitted with state-of-the-art medical equipment that allows the medical staff to provide Emergency Room level care.

The medical jet arrived in Miami well after midnight, I was transferred to an ambulance, transported to Baptist Hospital, and admitted into the Emergency Room. As the nurse was preparing me for a cardiac catheterization—a procedure where a catheter was inserted into my arm and threaded through blood vessels to my heart—a "code blue" alarm was sounded on the hospital's intercom system. Code blue indicates a life-threatening medical emergency, usually due to cardiac or respiratory arrest. I remember saying to my sister, who lives in Florida and met me at the hospital, *someone is in serious trouble.* The next thing I know, doctors and nurses poured into my room. The code blue alarm was for me!

My heart rate was close to 200 beats per minute and I needed to undergo another cardioversion—the second in two days. Despite the emergency, I remember how calm things seemed.

The doctors and nurses were in complete control. I was quickly sedated and the cardioversion was successfully completed.

I went on to spend the next ten days in the cardiac intensive care unit (ICU) where they ran all kinds of tests for infectious diseases, followed by testing, testing, and more testing. I was reasonably stable by this point, and was walking around the ICU every day, wondering why I was there and thinking I probably just needed some medicine. I had told my girlfriend Rhonda to stay in Aruba with her kids—I said I was just going to go and get checked out in Miami and that I'd be back down there to join them in a day or two. But that didn't happen. I hadn't really seen any progress, and didn't have any diagnosis, so I started pushing for a transfer to a hospital in Boston.

Initially, the doctors would not allow me to leave Baptist Hospital because they believed I was at risk of sudden death. After some heavy persuasion, they finally agreed to let me leave if I promised to do two things: 1) wear a LifeVest—a medical device designed to detect life-threatening heart rhythms and automatically deliver a shock to save a patient's life, and 2) carry a little card to get through airport security that says I'm at risk of sudden death and cannot remove the LifeVest. I couldn't take the vest off—it had a huge battery pack on the left side—but finally, with my vest on, I checked out of Baptist Hospital and left. I had to stay in a hotel by myself the first night, which truthfully freaked even me out a little. I'd been tethered to the hospital system for ten days, and now there I was—in a hotel room, alone—with nothing but my LifeVest to protect me. No doctors. No nurses. No monitors.

I couldn't fall asleep, and by two or three in the morning I had to give myself a speech. *Just stop it. Close your eyes, and get some rest,* I thought sternly. And so I did.

I woke up the next morning and hopped on an early flight, but I didn't fly directly to Boston. Remember, I was the CEO of a public company, and we had important meetings scheduled in New York: a Board of Directors meeting, Annual Shareholder meeting, and our first quarter earnings report to Wall Street. I figured that New York was technically on the way to Boston, so I stopped there for two days to lead the meetings. This seems like a terrible idea when you hear the rest of the story, but at the time I simply thought to myself, *I'm the CEO of a public company and people are counting on me. I have this LifeVest. I'm not going to die.* I proceeded to lead the meetings as if nothing was wrong—the LifeVest and battery pack with flashing red light neatly concealed by my suit jacket. I had to fulfill two more commitments before going to Boston. So, I drove to JFK airport to meet the CEO of one of our European distributors (who had flown from France to meet with me), and I drove to Connecticut to meet with a shareholder. Finally, I was on my way to Boston.

Upon my arrival in Massachusetts, Rhonda took me straight to Massachusetts General Hospital. This is where I wanted to be from the moment I arrived at the emergency room in Aruba. I knew Mass General was one of the best hospitals in the world, and the doctors and nurses are among the best in the business. I felt an immediate sense of relief as I entered the iconic front doors of the hospital.

Still wearing the LifeVest, I sat down with a cardiologist who specializes in heart failure. She said, "John, I've reviewed your medical records from the hospital in Miami, and you are showing signs of acute heart failure. It is serious and life-threatening. Treatment could range from surgery and medication—to the need for a heart transplant."

It's hard to even put that moment into words. I mean, there I was—a guy who had been an athlete his whole life. I trained every day. I don't drink, I don't smoke. I don't use drugs. And I might need a heart transplant? *You've GOT to be kidding.* If you had asked me to list a hundred things that might go wrong with me medically in my life, a heart transplant wouldn't have made the list. *Are you kidding me?* Any kind of heart issue isn't on ANYONE'S radar if there's no family history of anything like that. It was the furthest thing from my mind.

I was admitted to Massachusetts General Hospital and my first surgery occurred on day one. An implantable cardioverter defibrillator (ICD) was placed through an incision just below my left collarbone and wires, or leads, were connected to specific locations in my heart. The ICD responds to irregular, life-threatening heart rhythms. It corrects a fast rhythm and promotes a normal heartbeat by sending a shock (defibrillation) that resets the heart rhythm to prevent sudden cardiac arrest. My second surgery occurred on day three. An Impella pump was inserted into my heart to take over the blood pumping function of my left ventricle. My condition continued to deteriorate, so the doctors scheduled another surgery on day four—this time for a procedure called a heart tissue biopsy, where small pieces of heart tissue are removed for examination.

My fourth day at the hospital was a pivotal day. I remember my surgeon entering my room, walking to my bedside and explaining that the heart tissue biopsy provided a diagnosis. This was the moment I had anticipated since that first day in Aruba. Finally, I got to hear the answer to what was causing all of this. I listened intently, hanging on every single word, hoping for a simple explanation. He said, "John, you have giant cell myocarditis. It is very rare and very grave—you are going to be in the fight of your life."

I later learned that giant cell myocarditis is one of the world's rarest disorders. It was first discovered in 1905 and it has been diagnosed less than 300 times in medical history—and most of those were at autopsy. It is idiopathic, which means they don't know its origin (no known cause)—and unfortunately, the average time from diagnosis to death is about four months. The fact is, they don't catch very many people living with giant cell myocarditis, and when they do, a heart transplant is almost the only route to survival.

Massachusetts General Hospital had only seen one case of giant cell cyocarditis before me in over two hundred years. That's how rare it is. One of the top five hospitals in the world, and they've seen *one case*.

As I lay on my back in the ICU, I held my iPad above my face and researched Giant Cell Myocarditis—devouring every medical document I could find. I kept seeing the same name on article after article: Dr. Leslie Cooper at the world-renowned Mayo Clinic, who is an expert on giant cell myocarditis. I asked my team at Mass General, "Are you talking to Dr. Cooper at Mayo; he seems to be the leading authority on giant cell?" And they'd say, "John. We've got this. We're talking to everybody."

My response?

"OK, what's the game plan?"

"Well, we're going to put you on ECMO, a life support system designed to take some of the pressure off of your heart and try to increase your chances of survival. Technically, it's called veno-arterial ECMO."

I had spent nearly thirty years leading life science companies, so I knew of ECMO but I didn't know what it would be like as a patient. I went on to read that only the sickest of the sick are placed on ECMO. The majority of patients that are put on ECMO don't survive. For those that do survive, the next greatest risks are irreversible brain damage and limb death, due to lack of oxygenated blood to the extremities. At that moment, I remember being pretty focused on the risk of death, and didn't pay much attention to the other risks.

I asked the doctor what ECMO would be like as a patient, and I recall him saying that I wouldn't remember anything because I would be put into a medically-induced coma. My brain was processing all of this information. I have a rare and deadly disorder. I need a heart transplant. I'm going to be put into a coma and placed on life support. There is a risk of death. I am fighting for my life. As a CEO, I am used to processing information and making decisions; it's what I do every day. This was different—these decisions might determine whether I live, or die. I asked a question, "Instead of being put into a medically-induced coma, can I just stay awake while I'm on life support?" Gauging by my medical team's response, I don't think anyone's ever asked that at Massachusetts General Hospital. Or—as it turns out—probably anywhere.

"That's not the standard of care and not really something that's done," they said. And they desperately tried to talk me out of it. "It'll be a horrific experience, both physically and psychologically, John. And we strongly advise against it."

Never a guy to just accept things as they are, I said, "I understand that. But that's not really the question I'm asking. I'm asking you: technically, medically, *can* I do it?" I'd already made up my mind that if the answer was yes, then that's what I was going to do. My life was on the line and I wasn't about to take a nap—I was going to stay awake and fight. And they came back and said, reluctantly, "We talked to the guy who invented the technology at the University of Michigan, Dr. Bob Bartlett, and while he advised against it, medically it can be done. You will obviously be put out for the surgery, but then you would be able to wake up in recovery and remain awake from that point onwards."

Other people's will and opinions will take over and determine the natural shape of your life if you let it. But I wasn't going to let that happen, which is why I wanted to stay awake. I knew it would be horrific. If they were telling me not to do this, because it was going to be horrific, it probably truly would be. But I figured I'm either going to survive it and get better, or I'm not and it's going to be over. But at least I'll be awake and have a say in the matter, and it'll be my choice how the story ends.

CHAPTER 2

There was only one time during my time in the ICU where I actually thought *maybe this isn't survivable.* That was the fifteen minutes after I woke up from that surgery to put me on life support. I was laying flat on my back in my ICU bed. My arms and legs had been restrained so I could only move my head. I looked down at my body and under the thin sheet I saw tubes coming out of my torso and my groin. I could feel the weight of them, filled with my blood as it exited my body, circulated through the ECMO machines, and re-entered my body. I turned my head to the left and saw blood being transfused into me through another tube. I later learned the blood transfusion was necessary because ECMO hemolyzes, or destroys, the red blood cells. The feeling was physically and mentally overwhelming. I immediately realized why the doctors tried to talk me out of being awake while on life support, and what they meant by "horrific." I remember looking at Rhonda, who was sitting in a chair next to me, and saying, "As strong as I think I am, I'm not sure anyone can survive this."

But after those fifteen minutes, I got past it. Because I had to. I was in the fight of my life, and I had only one option if I wanted to survive: I had to fight. And that's what I did. I spent fifty-five days in the cardiac intensive care unit at Mass General, including eight excruciating days on life support. Normally ECMO is used as a very short bridge—one or two days (because it's very destructive to your vital organs)—but because I was a super healthy person, the doctors figured my other organs could handle it and they would recover, even if they pushed them to the wall of destruction. And they did.

I was completely engaged in the whole process. I was my own advocate, because I was awake. I could tell the doctors and nurses how I felt, and I could explain what was going on—and they could talk to me. I thought that was a huge advantage, but there was a little bit of psychology I was playing with as well. Doctors and nurses are human beings, too, and I figured if they saw I was willing to lay it all on the line like that—and do something almost unheard of—they'd be much more likely to fight harder for me, too.

I could also talk to my family members, who were there to visit me throughout my stay at Mass General. Having people in your corner when you're battling for your life—just knowing they are there—makes a huge difference.

By the eighth day of ECMO, my vital organs had been pushed to the wall and my long-term survival was at risk. I was scheduled for immediate surgery to take me off of life support and undergo a major heart surgery. I had my first sternotomy, where the surgeon cut open my chest, sawed through my sternum, and pried my ribs apart to get access to my heart. The surgeon implanted what's called a Left Ventricular Assist Device (LVAD) and a Right Ventricular Assist Device (RVAD)—collectively these are called a BIVAD, which basically takes over the function of your heart.

Once the LVAD is hooked up, it's portable. It has a drive line that comes out of your torso and circulates your blood from the left ventricle—the one that pumps the oxygenated blood throughout your body. The RVAD, on the other hand, is hooked up to a machine in the ICU which unfortunately meant I wasn't going anywhere. In my case, the BIVAD was required to (hopefully) keep me alive until a donor heart became available for transplant. This was going to be the last bridge to what we hoped would be the heart transplant I needed to save my life. There was no other alternative. If a donor heart didn't arrive in time, I wouldn't survive. It was, by pure definition, a binary outcome.

So there I was, my tenth day in the cardiac surgical intensive care unit. I had undergone four surgeries in ten days, including spending eight days on life support. I now had this BIVAD system controlling my heart function. There were tubes sewn into my torso, connecting the devices to my heart, moving blood throughout my body. Once again, I found myself being kept alive by medical devices. While my mind was strong, my body was already being put to a serious physical test. I was literally fighting for my life every single day. I had to stay focused on one thing—survival—but I also needed to keep my mind sharp. So, I worked every day from my hospital bed. I worked closely with the interim CEO, and communicated with the executive leadership team and board of directors. I wasn't trying to be a superhero, it was just to keep my eyes—and brain—focused on something else.

When you're in that spot and your life is entirely dependent on someone else—another person and another family—having a tragedy in order to save your life, it's a really hard thing to wrap your head around. One of the most difficult things I've ever had to get behind, in fact.

I was on the transplant waiting list, and I knew from what I had been reading that certain holidays are prone to accidents, which are more likely to cause donor organs to become available. The Memorial Day holiday was one of them. Memorial Day came and went. Nothing.

As I sat there in the hospital awaiting a transplant, engaging in the process and doing everything I could to stay strong, I got a hospital-acquired infection—pneumonia. When you stay in the hospital for an extended period, especially in the ICU, you become very susceptible to infections. I battled pneumonia for several days. It was a brutal experience. I couldn't breathe. I could barely open my eyes for two days, and I felt like I was drowning in my own fluids. I remember thinking, *I am not about to let pneumonia take me down.*

Then I got what became a life-threatening blood clot in my chest—outside my heart. Unfortunately, blood clots are one of the complications, or risks, associated with what I was going through. When the doctors first discovered the clot, they decided to leave it there, because it was not life-threatening and the only way to remove it was to perform another sternotomy—to cut open my chest through my breast bone a second time. And they were worried that I had become so weak that even IF a donor heart became available, I wouldn't survive a third sternotomy for the heart transplant. So they tried to put it off as long as they could.

But the day soon came when the doctor announced that the clot had become life-threatening and they would need to schedule immediate surgery to take it out the next day. And because I was awake and engaged, I could feel where I was on that spectrum. I knew I was at the edge of a very steep cliff. I asked him, "So what about a second sternotomy leading to a third? How do you feel about that?" He said, "We don't have that choice anymore. We will cross that bridge later."

Once again I found myself trying to wrap my head around yet another really tough thing. Going through a second sternotomy and getting this clot out was one thing, but then continuing to fight while hoping a donor heart becomes available, only to have another major surgery, could have a really grave outcome.

Shortly after I was diagnosed with giant cell myocarditis, I went through an evaluation process to determine whether I was a candidate for heart transplantation. The process included a full medical and dental evaluation, as well as meetings with the hospital's heart transplant coordinator, psychiatrist, physical therapist, nutritionist, and social worker. While the meetings were intended to evaluate me and my potential for transplantation, I used these meetings to learn from these experts and prepare myself mentally.

I vividly recall the psychiatric evaluation, which is designed to assess how I function emotionally and how I would be able to cope with the stress of a heart transplantation and recovery. As overwhelming as it might seem to imagine yourself in a hospital ICU—knowing that you need a heart transplant to survive—my meeting with the psychiatrist felt like the last piece of the puzzle I needed to prepare myself. The last thing he said before leaving my room was, "I will come see you each day while you're here." My response was, "Doc, I'm not sad. I'm not upset. I'm not asking 'why me?' Feel free to spend your time with other patients who *really* need you. I'm good. I've got this." And God bless him, he still came to my room every single day at five or six o'clock, and he would just sit there and just shoot the breeze about nothing related to what I was going through.

I didn't really get it at the time, but I do now. I understand now that he was there—that he *wanted to be there*—because maybe one day I would talk to him about something or I would have a concern.

And as I lay there in the ICU, mentally and emotionally processing the surgery I would have the next day, he appeared once again. He said, "John, all this time I have respected the fact you didn't want me to cross the imaginary line you've drawn between us, and I have honored the boundaries you put in place. I appreciate that, and haven't forgotten it. But I'm going to break that rule today."

"All right," I said. "You've earned the right. Give it to me."

"You're on a tightrope. Do not look down." That's all I remember him saying. What he was trying to tell me is that you're in a really tough spot, and you have to keep fighting. If you don't, you're going to have a bad outcome.

I said, "I know. My body is getting weak but I will keep fighting. I never give up." I could sense that we were getting close to the wire.

He was obviously in close connection with my doctors and nurses, and I'm guessing they didn't want to be the ones to tell me that.

Well, I'm not really the kind of guy who just takes one data point and considers it to be the gospel truth, so I decided to ask around. I had two nurses (a day nurse, and a night nurse) who were assigned to me on an ongoing basis, unless they had a day off. They were my nurses for the entire time for each of their shifts, and at the moment it was Laura who was working. Every day I would ask her, "How're we doing, Laura?" half joking and with a smile. She'd always say, "Oh, we're doing good."

This day, however, when I asked her, "Laura, how're we doing?" she said, "I'm worried, John. I'm *very* worried."

That was the moment I knew for sure.

When you're engaged with these folks every single day, for nearly two months, and one day they say, "I'm worried," you know it's because they know what it means and they know what the next thing looks like before it happens. And that's when you realize this isn't like a basketball game where, if you look up and see four minutes and twenty-two seconds left on the clock, you know you just have to make it four minutes and twenty-two seconds before you can catch your breath. This is different: this is where you have to just fight and fight and fight and fight and fight for your life. And you have no idea if you're going to fight for a week, or a month, or a year.

Luckily it wasn't too many hours that passed while I sat there thinking through all of this before my cardiac surgeon came back into the room and said, "I have some good news."

I said, "The clot isn't life-threatening anymore?"

He said, "No, the clot is still life-threatening. And we have to take it out. But... the good news is, John—we have a heart, and it's a *great* heart."

CHAPTER 3

I will remember that exact moment for the rest of my life—I still get goosebumps thinking about it.

The first feeling I had was one of sadness. *Somebody else lost their life in order for me to live.*

It was a few days earlier—on the weekend of the fourth of July—the next of the "more likely" holidays. It was that weekend that ultimately ended up being the one where someone had an accident—my heart donor had *his* accident— and I became the beneficiary of that incredible life-taking and life-giving tragedy.

I wouldn't go on to learn these details until much, much later, but Alex was a twenty-four-year-old schoolteacher studying to get his master's degree. He went up to the lake house with one of his friends for the fourth of July, and they did what I'm sure they've done a hundred times before: hopped on their skateboards and went down to the water. Only this time was different. In a freak accident, he fell off and—even though he had a helmet on—he had a traumatic head injury that was unrecoverable. And after a couple of days of being on life support, he didn't survive.

Rhonda had been there in the hospital with me literally every single day, and she later admitted when the doctors came in and told us there was a donor heart available, my reaction wasn't what she expected it to be.

It was because I felt sad. I felt sad because I realized that while my family was rallying for me to survive, someone else's family had been doing the exact same thing for their loved one—but for them the outcome was very different. I had thought about this scenario over and over while I waited for a donor heart.

My next thought was, *how am I ever going to express gratitude to that family?*

With all of these thoughts going through my mind, I remember them describing how all of the devices I had—the implantable cardiac defibrillator, the LVAD, and the RVAD, they were all coming out, along with the clot *and* my native heart.

I was a physically weak patient at this point; I had lost a lot of weight and most of my muscle mass. This was going to be a major surgery. Heart transplants are among the most complicated procedures, carrying great risk to the patient. Even just extracting all of those devices from my chest would be a pretty complicated surgery. As the doctors and nurses prepared to move me out of my ICU room and to the operating room, I remember saying to my surgeon, "Doc, I don't know how I'm going to deliver on this promise, but I promise you, if you save my life, I'll make you proud." As you can probably imagine, these cardiac transplant surgeons have so much swag and confidence; he just looked at me and said, very matter-of-factly, "It doesn't matter John. I'm going to save your life either way."

Now *that's* the guy I want operating on me. Yes, sir.

I was wheeled away, sedated, and the next thing I remember is waking up the next day, feeling fantastic.

They had sent my family home, saying that I was going to be out of it for a couple of days. But I woke up almost immediately, asking, "Where's my family? Let's get them in here! I feel great."

I looked at the EKG monitor, as I had so many times throughout my hospital stay, and had to ask if that was my heart rate. With my native heart and giant cell myocarditis, mine had looked like what a third grader would have drawn if you asked her to show you an EKG. This one was perfectly normal. Indeed, I had received a *great* heart.

I didn't feel any different than when I stepped into the hospital other than the wave of emotion that comes from knowing I had survived something so rare, and so deadly. And all because somebody made the choice, the selfless choice, to be an organ donor.

While in the ICU prior to the surgery, I started to notice I was losing sensation in my lower legs. It started in my toes and moved up toward my knees. First the right leg, then the left. It was a tingling sensation that reminded me of when I had stayed outside in the winter and my feet were nearing frostbite.

At a certain point, my lower legs turned black from the knees down. *Really black.* Rhonda noticed it and called the nurses in, and the nurses called the doctor in.

I had named both my brother and Rhonda as my two healthcare proxies when I was first admitted to the hospital. I told the doctors if something was relatively normal news that they should tell them both at the same time. But if something was really bad, they should tell my brother first and he could tell the rest of the family, including Rhonda. I didn't want Rhonda to have to deal with telling everyone really bad news, because I needed her to focus on just being there for me—to continue to be my rock.

When the doctor came in, he glanced at my legs, turned around, and as he started to walk back out of the room he said, "Yes, they're black. Put some socks on them, put a blanket over him, and stop looking at them. I'm trying to save his life."

While I don't remember saying it, apparently my response was, "Doc, if it's all the same to you, I'd like to keep my legs."

My brother eventually told me, six months later, "They called me when your legs turned black, and said they might have to amputate. I told them, 'Look, you already gave the guy almost no shot at survival; if my brother's going to die, he's going to die with his legs on.'"

While I *did* ultimately get to keep my legs, they no longer worked by the time they were preparing to discharge me from Mass General. I was confined to a wheelchair because I couldn't walk—I was weak and didn't have any feeling from the knees down.

They said to me, "You're going to need to go to an inpatient rehabilitation hospital to learn how to walk again."

I had known this was one of the potential risks associated with the life support system and all of the surgeries I'd had. They put these cannulas (tubes nearly the size of garden hoses) into your groin area to connect your venous system or your arterial system, which means you just don't get enough oxygenated blood to your extremities. Unfortunately this is just one of the possible outcomes, and I didn't fight it. I was alive, and I could do this: I could learn to walk again.

There was only one small obstacle-the rehabilitation hospital I wanted to go to didn't accept heart transplant patients. I wanted to go to Spaulding Rehabilitation Hospital, where many of the Boston marathon bombing victims went. It's a new, state-of-the-art facility on the waterfront in the old navy yard of Boston. It's both really progressive *and* really nice, and it felt like the place where I would have the best chance (and the most aggressive team available) to help me learn to walk again as soon as humanly possible.

I had to battle and fight, and become my own greatest advocate in order to get in, but eventually I got what I wanted. *Spaulding here I come.*

Just as I was about to make the move to Spaulding rehab, my temperature spiked.

When you've been in the hospital for as long as I'd been, you don't really pay attention to your temperature—even though they've been taking it multiple times a day for weeks. No news is good news, apparently—if it's not worth talking about, no one even mentions it, and they just record the number in your chart and move on.

But when it suddenly spikes and you are literally watching it skyrocket, it becomes immediately evident this is bad news.

The doctors came in and told me I had some kind of infection, but they didn't know what it was.

Even though I *felt* great, after the heart transplant I had lost forty pounds and I was obviously super weak. I was on immunosuppressants, which made me extremely vulnerable to other kinds of infections.

It started out feeling kind of like a urinary tract infection with a fever. But it ended up being a bacterial infection that you only get in a hospital—it's what's called a "hospital-acquired infection."

I didn't know much about hospital-acquired infections when I went into all of this—my knowledge about that space was quite superficial. I'd heard of MRSA, which I think everybody's pretty much heard of, but truthfully about all I knew was that it's bad and can lead to sepsis.

They started me on antibiotics right away. The treatment protocol included multiple broad-spectrum antibiotics delivered through an IV, with the bags needing to be changed out every two hours.

When you've gone through all that I had, and about to be mobile and free again, it was a huge blow to have them say, "Sorry, John. You're going to be stuck here, attached to this IV pole, for another ten days to complete the antibiotic treatment."

I knew there was nothing I could do, so if that's what I was going to have to deal with, then that's what I would have to deal with. Rehab would have to wait. I hunkered down with my IV pole, cracked open my laptop, and went back to work from my hospital bed.

While these high dose antibiotics are pretty rough on a person's system, they appeared to be doing their job. I think because I had really never been exposed to antibiotics before—I was always a perfectly healthy guy—my immune system responded to it. My temperature went down, and I got better after the ten-day course. I was done with the antibiotics, and I felt—and seemed—fine.

CHAPTER 4

It turned out to be worth fighting for—Spaulding Rehabilitation Hospital is a phenomenal place. It is the teaching hospital for Harvard Medical School's Department of Physical Medicine and Rehabilitation.

Upon arrival, when I asked the doctors how long it would take me to learn how to walk again, their answer was, "It could take several months, John."

My response was immediate, "I don't have several months. I only have two. And it would be better if I could do it in one."

"What are you talking about?" they said. "You just survived giant cell myocarditis and had a heart transplant—you need to give it time, as long as it takes."

By now I'm sure you've realized I'm a super competitive guy. While I was in the ICU, I was researching CEOs that had heart transplants, and whether a person could actually even come back into a public company CEO role after having a heart transplant. I read that Oscar Munoz, the Chairman of United Airlines, had a heart transplant and went back to work within a couple of months. The bar had been set (thank you Mr. Munoz). Right there, I set my goal. I decided I would go back to work, full-time in the New York offices, on Monday, October 2, 2017—the first day of our fourth quarter. It was an ambitious goal—to return faster than anyone would or could even imagine after all I had been through.

I didn't allow myself any extra buffer or grace to account for the magnitude of the ordeal I had gone through. Mine wasn't the standard case of having a heart problem, being placed on the transplant list, and living my normal life while waiting for a transplant (which is what happens most of the time). I was on the edge of death. I was on life support. It was a tough case, which is now well documented in the world's most prestigious peer-reviewed medical journal, the New England Journal of Medicine. None of that mattered to me at this moment—I was not prepared to use that as an excuse. I was focused on one thing, and one thing only: beating Oscar Munoz's record for the fastest time ever for a public company CEO to return back to work after a heart transplant. Only in that time, not only did I need to recover from the transplant, I also needed to learn how to walk again.

A few days in, I spiked another temperature.

Fortunately, Spaulding Rehabilitation Hospital and Mass General Hospital are both part of the same health system, so I was still within their network. Because the systems are all linked, the doctors realized they didn't get the bug out of my system the first time, so they needed to put me back on antibiotics a second time. This time they had to choose different ones, though, because the ones they put me on initially clearly didn't do the trick.

During this next ten-day course of high-dose antibiotic treatment (and stuck to the IV pole again) at least I could go outside if somebody pushed me out in my wheelchair—as long as the monitoring system didn't get out of range. It was amazing to finally get some sun and fresh air and to finally feel somewhat mobile, even if I still couldn't walk. Ten days later, I seemed fine, and we thought the bug seemed to be gone.

I worked incredibly hard during my rehabilitation at Spaulding. The doctors and physical therapists were incredible. They pushed me, and I pushed them to push me even harder. I got stronger every day, and I learned how to walk again without having any feeling from the knees down (which I still don't have today).

And I got out of there in *only* twenty-nine days because I was completely determined to do it. I set an ambitious goal and I worked hard each day to achieve it.

I was discharged from the rehab facility, and after all of this nightmare I *finally* got to go home.

I had spent ten days at Baptist Hospital, fifty-five days at Massachusetts General Hospital and twenty-nine days at Spaulding Rehabilitation Hospital. As I crossed the threshold into the house at 2pm on the day of my release, my first thought was, *the saga is over. I survived my diagnosis, I've got a new heart, I can walk again, I can resume my life and I can get back to work.* The next two hours were pure bliss. I hadn't felt this free since that fateful night in Aruba, when I went to bed and didn't wake up.

But by four o'clock that afternoon, my temperature was at 104 degrees—and rising.

I called the heart transplant center at Mass General Hospital, and they instructed me to get back to the hospital immediately.

We hustled back to Mass General, and I was readmitted to the intensive care unit once again because they were worried this could turn septic.

They took blood and sent it to the lab for a culture, and when they eventually got the results they realized it was a multi-drug resistant bacteria infection, often referred to as "ESKAPE pathogens."

The one I had was called *Pseudomonas aeruginosa*, and it's one of those really deadly hospital-acquired bacterial infections I had heard about before I left Mass General the first time.

I didn't know anything about pseudomonas—it was just a weird sounding word that I couldn't spell nor had ever heard of. The fact I had gotten it was just the craziest thing in the world to me.

I mean, you go to a hospital to get better, right? *Not* to acquire something that will make you even more sick—or potentially kill you.

I went on to learn that these fungal and bacterial pathogens exist in the hospital, and if you stay there long enough and have openings in your body, it's like saying, "OK, guys. Come on in." And that's what happened in my case.

I'd already won the statistical lottery twice—the first time being diagnosed with an incredibly rare and deadly disorder, and a second time receiving a heart transplant just in time to save my life. *Then* I almost lost both of my legs and had to learn how to walk again. And *now*—after all of the phases of near death I'd gone through—I might get taken out by some stupid, random deadly bacterial infection I caught from being in the hospital? *You have GOT to be kidding me,* I thought to myself.

It turns out this was *anything but* a joke.

ELEVEN MILLION PEOPLE AROUND THE WORLD DIE FROM SEPSIS EVERY YEAR—with 270,000 of those people dying every year in just the United States alone[1].

Think about that for a moment.

During the great worldwide pandemic of 2020, COVID-19 brought almost the entire planet to a standstill and killed more than 1.5 million people globally in *one* year. Sepsis kills

---

1   "Sepsis," Centers for Disease Control and Prevention (Centers for Disease Control and Prevention, December 7, 2020), https://www.cdc.gov/sepsis/datareports/index.html.

more people each year than all forms of cancer combined...
ELEVEN MILLION PEOPLE AROUND THE WORLD
EVERY YEAR.

The human toll related to sepsis is shocking, and yet so few
people seem to know anything about it. The economic toll
is equally shocking. According to the US government, sepsis
represents $62 billion in US healthcare costs each year.

Sepsis is a term many of us may have heard of before, but
we don't really understand what it actually means. It's a life-
threatening complication from an infection that occurs when
chemicals released in the bloodstream to fight an infection,
trigger inflammation throughout the body. This can cause
dangerously-low blood pressure and a cascade of changes that
damage multiple organ systems, impairing blood flow to organs
like the brain, heart or kidneys—which in turn can lead to
organ failure and tissue damage, and death.

Unlike other diseases or conditions, there is no single test for
sepsis. Doctors evaluate your symptoms, your history, and do a
series of blood tests like a CBC (complete blood count), lacate
(testing the level of lactic acid in your blood), CRP (C-reactive
protein), and a blood culture. While none of these tests can
definitively diagnose sepsis, when the test results are combined
with a physical examination and information about your illness
it leads them to _suspect_ you have sepsis.

The problem with this is twofold: timing, and margin for error.

One of the critical tests they do is called a blood culture, which tries to identify what type of bacteria or fungi caused infection in the blood. Blood cultures are generally effective at determining this *eventually*, but the unfortunate thing is that they take time—several days—to get the results because they grow the cultures in a petri dish.

The high speed at which the infection spreads, combined with the slow speed slow speed of getting the test results to tell you what actually caused it, is what makes sepsis so incredibly deadly. It's a ticking time bomb, and every hour it takes to figure out which strain caused it counts. For every hour a patient remains untreated or improperly treated, the risk of death increases by up to eight percent.

This timeline presents too great of a risk, so doctors begin treatment immediately using a ten-day course of multiple, heavy-dose, broad-spectrum antibiotics delivered through an IV, without *actually* knowing which bacteria or fungi they're actually fighting. And often—as in my case, too—it appears to work the first or second time, so they just keep treating you and only realize when it returns (or when a blood culture reveals which bacteria or fungi caused the infection), that they've been treating you with the wrong antibiotics for twenty or more days. And by blasting patients with these ten-day courses of heavy-dose antibiotics that aren't even the right ones for what they're trying to fight, we're literally creating a world of antibiotic resistant superbugs. This is a HUGE problem.

Later, when I was telling my story to the CEO of a hospital system (who began her career as a cardiac surgical intensive care unit nurse) she said, "Speaking as a former nurse and a hospital CEO, John, do you realize how many death sentences you got along the way?"

"Yeah, I know there were several," I said with a smile.

"The bacterial infection you got at the end, after the transplant—we literally refer to that within the hospital as 'the kiss of death.'"

I knew it was bad, but I had never heard it characterized that way. And that really gave a different meaning and perspective to it.

It was hard to believe, after everything I had been through, that *a bacterial infection could turn septic and* might actually be the thing that would ultimately kill me. That of all the things I had survived, this hospital-acquired bug is the one that medical professionals fear most and label as the "kiss of death."

Days later, once the blood culture results eventually came through and the doctors knew which bacteria caused the infection, they were finally able to get me on the right antibiotics. After my third ten-day course, they finally killed the bug, and I was discharged. Again. And this time, it was for the last time.

It wasn't until much later that I learned my infection had actually become septic; I found out when I was digging through my medical record. In fact, the words seemed to jump off the page: "sepsis due to *Pseudomonas aeruginosa.*"

CHAPTER 5

When you become the recipient of an organ transplant, you receive information that explains the process you'll go through if you ever want to contact your donor's family.

I think it's probably similar to the way adoption was early on: a "blind" process where you are allowed to send a letter to the donor's family by way of a third party. The organization—in my case it was New England Donor Services—acts as a conduit between the two families. You have to send your letter to the organization, unsealed, so they can read it and make sure it complies with the rules. And it's recommended that you don't send it right away.

"Give it nine months," they said, "so the family can go through the grieving process." *Makes sense*, I thought, *but nine months feels like a very long time.*

I wrote my letter over the course of two months, and when I finished and reread it, I thought it was actually pretty good. I mean, I'm probably more of a math guy than an English guy, but I still thought it was pretty good.

Once it was written, I had to wait before I could send it. And as time went on, I kept reflecting. One day I had the thought, *I'm going to go online and just see if there are any letters out there to see how people express themselves within the parameters they give you.* It has to be somewhat generic, and you can't say much about yourself, and there are all of these rules about what you can and can't write in these initial letters to your donor family. I searched online, and the first letter I found was written by a woman who is a songwriter and a musician, and was the recipient of a double lung transplant.

I read her letter, and I instantly realized *my letter sucked. It's a terrible letter! It's way too generic!*

She inspired me immensely, and I completely rewrote my letter while still following the rules and the boundaries. *Now,* I thought to myself, *I have a way better letter. This is much better. I'm so glad I looked.*

But I still had to sit on it because I had to let the process happen and wait the nine months.

Then one day I got a call from Mass General Hospital saying they had a letter for me from my donor's family.

My first thought was, *Damn it! I wanted to give my letter to them first, because it just felt disrespectful for them to contact me first. What happened to the nine month waiting period?*

I went to Mass General, got the letter, and decided not to open it until I was with Rhonda because even though I'm not a crier, I *knew* I was going to cry. How could I not?

I sat down with Rhonda, and we read the letter together. It was beautiful, and *very* personal—written by a mom and a sister. They referred to him—to my donor—as "Alex." All of the emotions I felt when my doctor said, "We have a heart," came flooding back, returning me to the moment when I was sitting in the hospital bed thinking about someone else going through this tragedy in order for me to survive.

My next thought was, *my letter sucks. Again.* I knew I needed to make more changes to my letter to make it even more personal while still following the rules. *But how?*

Finally I thought, *this is absurd.*

I picked up the phone and called New England Donor Services and said, "I got a letter from my donor family."

"Yeah, we know, John—we were the ones who forwarded it to you."

"Can I please just send the family a letter that's more personal and give them my contact information?"

"It's not really something that's done," they said. And they tried to talk me out of it. "We'd like you to follow the process, John, and we would really prefer it if you didn't try to go outside the rules." It was similar to the phrase my doctors had used when I asked to remain awake on life support.

And in typical fashion I said, "Yeah, I *know*. I get all of that, but can I just do it?"

They went on to say that they were looking to get to a point where they could be a little more open about it, so they said, "Send us the letter and we'll take a look. If we're okay with it, we'll send it off."

I wrote down my name, included my email address and phone number, and sent them my letter—hoping the family would get it and answer me back directly. Three or four months went by... nothing. I started to wonder if maybe they just wanted to have some closure on their side by telling me something about Alex and perhaps that was that?

After several months I received a card and a picture of Alex in the mail, along with a little stone with some engraving on it. The note shared how Alex had liked to travel and that the family had given these stones to all of his friends to bring with them when they travel—and I've done so on every trip since.

And then, an email connection started to happen. And then we agreed to meet at their house.

In the meantime, I had been asked to tell my story for the American Heart Association. They had a producer and videographer come in, and he did a fantastic job capturing my story in the form of a video, and the American Heart Association used it at a gala in New York to help fundraise. I decided to bring my laptop to that first meeting at their house, and had the video loaded up and ready to play. But I just didn't know how the meeting would go, or if they would even want to look at it—it was a difficult thing to anticipate.

His mom and dad (Pam and Peter) were there, and his sister, Emily, too—she was two years older than Alex, and they loved to travel together. His family told me the story of his life, and then they told me the story of his death:

"Passionate, smart and funny are the adjectives I would use to describe Alex if I could choose only three," his mom Pam recounts. "But I'm certain he was one of the most interesting and thoughtful people I will ever have known. It wasn't until after he had passed that I realized that Peter, Emily and I had all lost our best friend. He had a way of making each of us feel understood and appreciated. He intuitively knew how to 'best handle' all of us in our worst moments. He could turn around anyone's bad mood, and made me struggle to hold back laughter when I was so fuming mad that the last thing I wanted to do was laugh!

"Alex accepted everyone for what they were. He didn't have to agree with your politics or opinions to respect you. He respected everyone, gave everyone the benefit of the doubt and was a master devil's advocate. He patiently explained things to me over and over, wanting me to understand, whether it was a penalty call I didn't agree with while watching football, or how the Electoral College might affect the outcome of the election as results trickled in. Somehow he seemed to retain everything he'd read or heard. He had an amazing wealth of information. He knew crazy statistics from nearly every sport as well as the social, environmental, cultural and political happenings in every corner of the world. I attribute this to the fact that he was compassionate, but also a thoughtful listener. When you spoke to him, you felt heard; he always listened intently and reflected before responding.

"Alex was always in the process of reading multiple books, most recently, the *Game of Thrones* series, a biography on Che Guevara, H.P. Lovecraft's *Great Tales of Horror*, *For Whom the Bell Tolls*, *Brave New World*, *The Idolatry of God*—and these are just the ones I know of.

"He followed all sorts of media resources and was a monthly supporter of NPR. He was constantly observing, absorbing and contemplating something.

"Alex connected with everyone. His high school and college friends often had interests that were very different from his. At family gatherings (there were many with lots of cousins, aunts, uncles, etc.) Alex talked to everyone. He'd play Candyland with his young cousins, have in-depth discussions with his aunts about politics, argue the latest NFL trade with his uncles and then sit with his grandmother and talk about everything under the sun.

"It's an understatement to say that Alex was a football fan. He went to his first New England Patriots game when he was about seven years old and closely followed the NFL as well as college football. He played youth football through high school, never a star player—he just loved the sport. He maintained a huge collection of cards and other collectibles. He also coached youth football for two years. In addition to football, Alex played the cello from the age of eight through high school. Like his talent for football, he didn't care about being the lead player. He just liked it and once he started something he was never quick to give it up. Alex was never big on change, which is ironic because he tried lots and lots of new things. He loved to kayak, hike, rock climb, play board games or poker with his friends, play tennis, chess, go fishing; he was always busy, but never too busy to spend time with us. He was the one who would stop and listen to a new piece of music with me, or come to look at the moon or stars if I said, 'Hey, come see this you guys.' He was generous with his time and whatever he had. He didn't need much. I would often try to buy him new clothes, sneakers— show him things online that I thought he'd like to have. But most often he'd politely decline, saying, 'Nah, I'm good.' Once, as he packed his things to go back to college after a weekend at home, I asked if he needed some money. 'No, I'm all set,' he said. His sister Emily sternly said, 'Alex, when Mom and Dad ask if you need money, the answer is always yes!'

"Alex had a close-knit group of friends through high school. They gathered every Friday night to play board games or poker and watch movies. After college, when many of them moved back home, they resumed this tradition of gathering up the street at his good friend Kevin's house on Friday nights. On weekends they'd hike or play football or spike ball. One of their friends was involved in theatre during high school; they always went to see his plays. Later, as this friend made a career of acting, they would travel all over the state to see him in plays.

"He loved video games, movies and music. Like his taste in books, his taste in music was hugely varied. He loved Pink Floyd, Bob Dylan, Lynyrd Skynyrd, Josh Groban, Andrea Bocelli, and musical soundtracks from *Les Miserables*, *Phantom of the Opera* and *Hamilton* which became a huge favorite of Alex and his friends. He got us all hooked. He was known to sing at the top of his lungs everything from 'You Raise Me Up' by Josh Groban to 'Umbrella' by Rihanna. The last CD he played in his car was Three Dog Night.

"After high school, Alex went to Stonehill College. He graduated with a degree in Psychology and Criminology. During college, he was required to participate in a semester of service. Alex tutored with School on Wheels, an organization that provides tutoring and mentoring for kids of all ages who are living in shelters, motels, foster homes. The experiences there seemed to affect Alex, and I think it was during this time that he began to see a future working with kids, and also when he gained deep compassion for those who struggle or live on the edge. He continued to volunteer after his commitment was fulfilled.

"After graduation, in 2015, Alex began working for Lawrence, MA public schools as a building-based educator. Lawrence is one of the poorest cities in MA and the population is largely Hispanic/Dominican. The job was sort of a combination of teaching assistant, mentor, and substitute when needed. He worked at the Hennessey School, Kindergarten through Grade

2. It was a great match. He connected with the kids and staff right away. To say that Alex went the extra mile at his job is an understatement. He would buy beginner books in English and Spanish so the students could help him with his Spanish while he helped them with their English. He voluntarily stayed late every day until the last student was picked up because he didn't want them to be left to wait in front of the principal's office, as if they were being punished. It seemed he befriended everyone from the principal and teaching staff, to the custodial staff and students. He cared deeply about the kids and would often buy things they needed and give them to the students' teachers to be discreetly passed on. During this time, Alex became familiar with the Boys & Girls Club of Lawrence. He often spoke of the great opportunities they provided for the kids of Lawrence. Tens of thousands of dollars have been raised for the club in his honor since he passed.

"After two years with Lawrence Public Schools, Alex decided to continue his education with a plan to become a school psychologist. He was elated when he was accepted into the school psychologist program at William James College— although he passed before starting this chapter of his life.

"On the hot, sunny morning of Wednesday, July 5, 2017, Alex left the house to go to our family cottage in Alton Bay, NH. The cottage is a big, very old house that his grandparents purchased in 1969. It's a rustic summer place where we've had family gatherings with extended family for years. Alex loved it there.

"On several occasions Alex would go up with a couple of friends, or by himself, for a few days of hiking, lake fun and solitude. On this day, his friend Matt from Stonehill was going with him. As they left the house holding their mason jars of coffee with soy milk, I told them to have fun and we waved goodbye. Two hours later I got a text from Alex: 'Arrived!' it said. 'Wonderful! Stay safe,' I replied, and I drove to my mother's for a visit.

"As I sat having tea with Alex's grandmother, my cell phone rang and I saw an incoming call from Alex. That was odd—he'd usually text. It was Matt on the other end when I answered. There had been an accident. Alex fell while they were skateboarding. He was being taken to the hospital. The next thing I knew I was speaking to the police chief who was asking questions about Alex's medical history. He would be medflighted to Dartmouth Hitchcock Hospital. Peter and I drove the two hours mostly in silence. We called Emily. She would ride up with my sister.

Over the next twenty four hours it became clear that Alex was not coming back to us. Family and friends arrived. At some point, a woman from New England Donor Services came to us. Alex, she said, was an organ donor. We knew this but it wasn't something that was on our radar. Alex had committed to being an organ donor when he got his license as a teen. There was no question—we would follow Alex's wishes. We were then led through a detailed list of potential organs that could be donated. One by one, organs were named and we were asked for a yes or a no. Peter, Emily and I agreed—if there was a chance that someone could benefit, we were for it, to say the least.

"We continue to learn things about Alex. Last year, after his grandmother's passing, I found several letters she had saved—letters Alex had written to her during college. I had found several cards and notes she had sent to Alex when going through his things. That wasn't surprising; she often sent notes to her grandchildren, and they always included money. But I had no idea Alex wrote letters back. It shouldn't have been a surprise.

"Alex appreciated life, nature, culture, travel, science, philosophy, history. But most of all he appreciated people. He was always true to himself. He lived each day fully and happily. We are still learning from him, and he will always be part of us."

We were there for five hours, and we went through the full range of emotions. It went from storytelling, to crying, to laughing, to sharing the similarities he and I have—and we started to make all of these little "connections."

Before the meeting, for example, Rhonda and I realized we had bought these little bracelets for all the nurses and the female doctors at Mass General that I had given out after the transplant. They all had a little red heart on them, symbolic of my new heart and the important work they do in the cardiac unit, and even though we didn't know his name was Alex at the time we bought them, the store where we got the bracelets from was called *Alex and Ani*—wow. We brought one for his mom and one for his sister to the meeting, and we told them the story, and we all started crying again.

During the meeting, his family would refer to his heart as "my" heart. And I kept saying, "You know, this is Alex's heart, and our families are bound forever through this." I knew his dad had been an EMT early in his career, and as a gift for him—instead of one of the bracelets—we bought him a really nice stethoscope. At one point during the meeting, I said to his mom, "Do you want to listen to Alex's heart?" She literally almost dove over the table, and I opened up my shirt and Alex's dad put the stethoscope on me, knowing exactly where to put it. Talk about emotions. As an organ, the heart is just so special to receive. A kidney or a liver is obviously life-changing to receive, too, but it's just different. With the heart, *you can hear it*. I mean, again, I'm not typically a crier, but I needed a case of water after that to rehydrate because the gravity of these moments we were sharing was so enormous.

I told his dad, "Alex and I are on this journey together now. There isn't a day that goes by that I don't think about and acknowledge that he saved my life. When he was sixteen years old, he checked the little box on his driver's license that said 'I want to be a donor.' And that's a heck of a lot more courageous than I was at sixteen years old. I certainly wasn't thinking about things like that at that age. And in fact, I wasn't even a donor until I was sitting in the hospital bed in the ICU. And I don't know if it's because I was too selfish, or I was uninformed, or I was ignorant about it, or all of the above, but the fact is—I wasn't. So right then and there, in the ICU, I signed up and became a donor. It takes five minutes. But this was a guy who did that at sixteen years old. And while there are not a lot of certainties in life, I am absolutely certain that his decision to do that saved my life."

I'm not a super religious guy. I don't go to church. But, I think I got giant cell myocarditis for a reason. I really believe that. Because come on—out of seven billion people in the world, it's diagnosed *a couple of times a year*. The chances of getting what I got are less than winning the Powerball jackpot. And then I won a *second* lottery by getting a heart transplant. On that Thursday in early July, they told my brother I may not survive past Saturday. That's right: they told him that on *Thursday*, and the transplant happened on Saturday. Alex's heart literally saved my life in the nick of time.

Alex's family and I have maintained a relationship since that very first meeting—sometimes by email, and other times in person. As a family, they've gone through an unimaginable grieving process. One of my sons was born in the same month and year as Alex, and as a father I can't fathom—even after knowing them and their situation so intimately—what they have gone through. I think if I were in their shoes it would be very hard to see and interact with me, but they've told me it gives them an incredible sense of relief and closure, and that they just felt so much better after meeting me, knowing that Alex's heart went to someone who would make such great use of it.

I take that very seriously. I recognize I'm not just living *my* life—I'm living Alex's life, and I'm also living the lives for the two other people who were on the heart transplant list but who didn't get a heart and died.

I think about it a lot: *I'm living for four people now.*

Some people would think of that as a weight, but I think it's an incredible gift, and I'm the lucky one to have gotten it.

And with the privilege of this gift comes great responsibility.

I am crystal clear that my purpose—my job on this planet—is to use this gift of life I've been given. To extract out of it all the lessons I've learned, to pay it forward, and help you—and others—to live YOUR life as the incredible gift it really is.

What follows are my "lessons for living." The key principles I've gleaned through my experience as a survivor—or better yet, *thriver*—medically, in sports, business, and life. May they serve you and support you, and guide you along your own path to becoming the best version of yourself you can be.

ALEX COE SAVED MY LIFE.

WHAT CAN YOU MAKE POSSIBLE?
TO REGISTER AS A DONOR, PLEASE VISIT
WWW.DONATELIFE.NET/REGISTER

PART TWO

LESSONS FOR LIVING

CHAPTER 6

HARD WORK

"Hard work beats talent if talent doesn't work hard." | Tim Notke

In my early days as a college quarterback, I often looked at other quarterbacks on the roster and thought to myself, *that guy is faster than me. That guy has a better arm than me, and that guy is a better athlete than me.* It didn't take me long to realize that ultimately those things were not going to determine who played on Saturday. I decided that my **thing** was that I could (and would) *outwork every single one of them.* That became my mindset on the football field, and it has continued to be a driving thought throughout my business life. Even now as the CEO of a public company, it's the decision to be the hardest worker on the team that drives my days.

Most CEOs of public companies didn't go to public high schools and state universities; they went to Ivy League schools and they have master's degrees. I made sure it didn't matter that I went to a public high school and a state college—I just flat out worked harder than anyone I met—in school, in sports, in business… everywhere. The notion of outworking the other person (or outworking the other company) became part of who I am.

It should come as no surprise to hear I learned this firsthand at home throughout my childhood years. So much of what we learn as kids is being modeled through behavior we witness by those around us in our formative years. As such, everyone's definition of hard work will be shaped by their own life and experiences.

I grew up in a military family—which means a lot of different things to a lot of different people. To some people that means we must have moved a lot; to other people, it means we must have grown up with a lot of structure and discipline. And I would say generally both of those were true. We didn't move as many times as a lot of military families (which is every three years or so) but we lived in a lot of different places, nonetheless.

Structure and discipline were requirements in our house. Things had to get done. My dad was in the Navy, every three years he would be on shore duty (working from the local base) followed by three years of sea duty—which meant every year he was away for six months. During those long months of sea duty, my mom was the only parent at home, raising four kids while working full-time in a doctor's office. She shuffled the four of us around to different schools and numerous sports, and then drove ten miles in the opposite direction to get to work on time. She epitomized hard work and she sacrificed a lot.

Throughout my adolescence, we lived on a horse farm, and everybody had things they had to do. If you have animals, you can't skip feeding them. And you can't skip cleaning a horse's stall. It just has to be done, and has to become part of your routine and part of your day. Plain and simple: it was a lot of hard work.

We often hear people say, "I work smart, so I don't have to work hard." Well, I'm here to tell you—successful people do both. They work smart *and* they work hard. I've never seen a successful person that didn't work hard.

If you try to look up hard work in the dictionary, however, you won't find it. You'll see things that are *like* hard work—effort, for example—but when it comes time to articulate what the core components of hard work really are, it's not there. On some level we all know and agree that hard work is important, and we know it when we see it. We know what extraordinary effort looks like, and we know what a lack of effort looks like. But what actually goes into hard work?

I believe there are a handful of key elements, which form a 5-step process:

1. Set a goal
2. Plan and prepare
3. Practice how you play
4. Put forth your best effort
5. Debrief: evaluate, review, and get feedback

STEP ONE: SET A GOAL

Have you ever seen those little bugs that zip around on the surface of the water? They look like they are going everywhere, but they're actually going nowhere. This is an important distinction to make when it comes to having a goal.

I spent a lot of time sitting in hockey rinks, watching my son as he climbed through the USA Hockey ranks. As I watched the tryouts, I would try to figure out where I thought my son fit in the group. I remember saying to another dad, "Wow, that number twenty-two is really an incredible skater. He's everywhere." To which this dad replied, "Don't confuse motion with action."

It was the perfect description of that particular player—he burned a tremendous amount of energy and he was very visible on the ice. He was seemingly everywhere, but he was accomplishing nothing. It's not enough to just exert effort. You need to know WHY, and for what—your effort needs to be directed. What are you working hard *toward*?

Renowned American philosopher Elbert Hubbard realized, as far back as the late nineteenth century, that many people failed in their endeavors—not because they lacked intelligence or courage, but because they didn't organize their energies around a goal.

This idea of organizing one's efforts to improve your chances of success was important, but it wasn't until the late twentieth century that George T. Doran, a consultant and former Director of Corporate Planning for the Washington Water Power Company published a paper titled, "There's a S.M.A.R.T. Way to Write Management's Goals and Objectives,"[2] which appeared in the November 1981 issue of *Management Review*.

Doran's original acronym provided five criteria (although, as he states, "the suggested acronym doesn't mean that every objective written will have all five criteria"):

- **Specific:** target a specific area for improvement
- **Measurable:** quantify, or at least suggest, an indicator of progress
- **Assignable:** specify who will do it
- **Realistic:** state what results can realistically be achieved given available resources
- **Time-related:** specify when the result can be achieved.

---

2   G.T. Doran, "There's a S.M.A.R.T. Way to Write Management's Goals and Objectives" (Scientific Research Publishing, 1981), https://www.scirp.org/(S(351jmbntvnsjt1aadkposzje))/reference/ReferencesPapers.aspx?ReferenceID=1459599.

In current day, the acronym has been expanded to include two additional criteria, making them S.M.A.R.T.*E.R.* goals:

- **Evaluated:** appraisal of a goal to assess the extent to which it has been achieved
- **Reviewed:** reflection and adjustment of your approach or behavior to reach a goal

I can't overstate the importance of having a goal. Goals are one of the keys to success in life, regardless of what industry or sport or field you're in—or even if you aren't actively working anywhere at all.

Inherent in the term "goal setting," or the phrase "set a goal," is the word set. And that word is of critical importance. As defined, the verb *to set* means "to put, lay, or stand something in a specified place or position." It doesn't just imply intentionality, it commands it. You SET a goal. You craft it. You place it. And then you put it in the foreground of your vision and you go for it.

But before you fly into action, you need to be strategic. And that begins with the next step in the hard work process: Planning and Preparation.

STEP TWO: PLAN AND PREPARE

Preparation and planning are another two terms we use all the time without much—if any—thought, and we rarely (if ever) take the time to look them up and really focus on what they mean.

Planning, as defined by Wikipedia, is the "process of thinking about the activities required to achieve a desired goal. It is the first and foremost activity to achieve desired results."

Preparation, on the other hand, is the "action or process of making ready for use or consideration, or something done to get ready for an event or undertaking."

While we often say "preparation and planning" when we use them together, in truth we've got them in the wrong order. And while we tend to use the two terms interchangeably in everyday life, when you read the definitions you realize they are actually two totally different things.

So first you plan, and then you prepare.

Let's dive in.

PLANNING

Both Warren Buffett and Bill Gates are well known for intentionally creating two hour blocks of time *per day* solely for the purpose of reading and thinking.[3]

If two of the world's richest people value thinking time as one of their greatest assets, it's probably something we can all stand to do a little more of ourselves.

---

3   Ryan McDaniel, "What Warren Buffett Taught Bill Gates about Managing Time by Sharing His (Nearly) Blank Calendar," Vimeo, January 25, 2021, https://vimeo.com/305482736.

Rhonda's son is a football player and he broke his leg at the end of his senior year in high school. It was significant enough to require surgery, and it impacted his ability to physically train before his freshman year in college. He decided that while he couldn't physically prepare, he would get ready for his return to the field by studying the playbook and having Zoom meetings with his coach. I checked in with him to ask how it was going and he said, "It's a different language. These are more complicated, offensive schemes." I encouraged him to keep at it, because I knew what he was studying was going to mentally set the foundation for his success when he returned to the field. When he stepped on the field again, it wouldn't be about whether he was a good athlete or not, but whether he actually had the knowledge to focus on executing the play. By not having to expend the mental energy to remember what the quarterback's calls mean in the moment, he could instead instantly know it, dive in, work hard, and execute.

I, too, was a football player (a quarterback) in high school and college. The whole week leading up to a game, we'd watch game tape of the other team, analyzing our opponent. We'd look at their defensive tendencies and then go out and practice our offense so that when we got to the game, it was easy to go out and execute. We almost didn't have to think about it, it was practically second nature.

If you approach business, your job, and your life the same way, you're much more likely to be successful—even in a crisis. Taking time to think about things and plan in advance, arm yourself with knowledge and information, and run a number of different scenarios and potential outcomes will create much greater success in any endeavor.

PREPARATION

ABRAHAM LINCOLN ONCE SAID, "IF I HAD EIGHT HOURS TO CHOP DOWN A TREE, I'D SPEND SIX SHARPENING MY AXE."

Preparation is one of the most important things you do to make your goals and hard work worthwhile. In business, life or sports, you play the way you prepare.

Each evening before I leave the office, I set my objectives for the next day. This allows me to assess how the day has gone and to prepare for what I need to accomplish the next day. When I walk into the office the next morning, I'm able to review what I set as my key priorities for the day ahead. I know which ones have carried over from the day before so I can quickly reassess to make sure that when I start the day, the plan is relevant. I quickly reassess to make sure that when I start today, the plan is relevant. Sometimes my plan gets derailed and I have to make changes, but spending time each evening planning and preparing for the next day provides me with a focus for my efforts.

If you plan and prepare, you're going to accomplish a lot more in life. If you wake up every morning and have a list of objectives you want to accomplish that day (or set them before you go to bed the night before) it becomes a powerful habit. You might not get them all done every day, but you're much more likely to see progress compared to showing up each day with a blank piece of paper, not knowing what you're trying to accomplish and/or not knowing where you're going.

STEP THREE: PRACTICE HOW YOU PLAY

What would your expected outcome be if you showed up to practice and only gave it a half effort? If you only ran at half speed, or focused on understanding only parts of the game? That partial effort from practice may be all you're capable of at the key moment when you need to be at full performance. You can't practice halfway and then expect to compete successfully at full speed. It doesn't translate; you have to practice exactly the way you plan to play. You need to practice with excellence so that when it's time to execute, it feels natural. It's a simple concept; if you want to run faster, practice running fast. We've all heard the expression *practice makes perfect*. A better way to say it is *perfect practice makes perfect*.

This same principle can be applied to any area of your life where you wish to find success. Proper planning and preparation, combined with relentless practice is a lethal combination. And the latter is what I believe truly sets some people apart from others when it comes to greatness: practice, practice, practice. And that's the part most people don't do enough of.

But why is practice so important?

Because practice equals preparation and preparation improves performance. It's irrefutable. *That's* why people practice—first to get better—and then, to become the BEST.

I'm often told on business calls that I'm a very natural speaker—but the truth is, I'm not a born orator. Sure, I'm confident speaking publicly but I've also practiced (and practiced, and practiced some more). I try to anticipate the questions somebody might ask, and I'm prepared to answer them to the best of my ability. I might not get every single one, but at a minimum I have spent the necessary time to be absolutely sure in my information set, so that when I need to recall it, I can do so without skipping a beat.

I would never get on a call with our whole organization without spending time preparing my remarks. I would never choose to just wing it, because there is absolutely no substitute for being well practiced and prepared. Can you imagine what it would have been like if my heart surgeon just walked into the operating room without reading my chart or doing any preparation? Many people may say, "Well that's heart surgery. That's different. That's life or death." What I'm asking is for you to give yourself and your life the respect it deserves, and treat it as though what YOU'RE doing has the same level of importance—that it is life or death. (Because it is.) Today could be your last day on the planet. Make every moment count.

STEP FOUR: PUT FORTH YOUR BEST EFFORT

One of the greatest lessons my dad instilled in me, is that effort doesn't cost anything—it's just effort. "Do your best," he'd say. That's an incredibly important motto. Because it's not always about being the best, but it *is* always about doing your best. Not everyone is an A student, but everyone can give an A effort.

And it's not just a little bit of preparation and practice. It's *relentless* preparation and practice. It's not just effort. It's your *best* effort. In sports we say, "Win the shift," or "Leave it all on the field." The point is, don't save anything. No matter what you're doing, you need to give it all you've got.

This even includes rest and recovery. In order to sustain high performance, you need to build in recovery rituals and rest so you don't burn out. So when it's time to rest, *REST.* When it's time to practice, *PRACTICE.* When it's time to play, *PLAY.* Full out. In life, don't do anything halfway.

And when it's game time, remember, you can't prepare for everything.

Like anything I undertake, I did absolutely everything I could to prepare when it came time to meet my heart donor Alex's family for the first time. I researched and I planned and I sought to understand what other people's experiences were like. I read some remarkable stories, I brought meaningful gifts, and going in I thought I was fully prepared. But as soon as I sat down with them at that first meeting, I realized that there are times in life you just can't fully prepare for. And that was definitely one of them. No amount of preparation could've ever readied me for the emotions I felt, the connection we shared, and the magnitude of the experience.

And that is one of the greatest gifts in life that preparation and practice gives you: the ability to let go in the moment and be fully present for the experience. To be able to live full out, and let go of everything else, aside from playing the game the best way you can in any—and every—moment. And the confidence to trust that as long as you're giving it your absolute best in that moment, it's absolutely perfect... no matter how things look or turn out (which includes crying your eyes out in front of your donor family).

And that—to me—is really what life is all about.

STEP FIVE: DEBRIEF—WATCH "GAME TAPE," REVIEW, AND GET FEEDBACK

Just like the "ER" in S.M.A.R.T.*E.R.* goals, evaluating and reviewing—debriefing—is a hugely important part of the process. We may have even saved the best for last.

In the same way it's difficult to be a great driver without the aid of a rearview mirror, it's tough to play your best game in life without taking time to reflect, review, get feedback, assess, and debrief.

If you've ever listened to a public company CEO report their quarterly results, there are two parts: scripted remarks, and a question & answer period with the analysts. I'm very involved in writing the scripted remarks—because I want it to be in my own words—and 'm the one who has lived through what's happened in the past three months. It would be really easy to just rehearse it a couple of times, jump on the call, read the scripted comments, and go confidently into the Q&A portion. It turns out when I've talked to some of my peers, that's what they do. I'm shocked by it. But that's what a lot of people do. They take the easy route. The hard route is what I prefer, and what many other successful people do, too— we rehearse it dozens of times. I mean *relentlessly* rehearse it. And I record it each time I rehearse, I time the scripted remarks with a stopwatch, and I listen to myself and critique my performance. That all happens *before* I actually hold the earnings call. And on game day, when I actually deliver it live, I've already practiced it so many times that it's natural and second nature. And through that repetition and refinement, it's become exponentially better.

And it doesn't stop there.

As a corporate athlete at the helm of a great team playing in the big leagues as a publicly traded company, I feel it is my duty—my obligation—to deliver the best performance for us and our shareholders. And so after the earnings call, that's when the planning and preparation begins for the next call. And it begins with the debrief.

Watching the game tape of the live call, evaluating and reviewing my own performance, and getting feedback from others are all critically important parts of the process. And it needs to be 360 degree feedback, including getting feedback from other people. If you've planned and prepared, and relentlessly practiced, you likely won't see your own blind spots but someone else may see a glaring weakness. Receiving constructive criticism is notoriously uncomfortable for everyone, but it needs to be done. It's imperative.

And so is laying down your ego in service of improving. If you can't receive honest feedback with grace and humility (in the spirit of growing and learning) you won't ever improve. And if you're not coachable, it's hard to become the best you can be.

And if you're not aiming to become the best version of yourself, what ultimately is the purpose of your life?

CHAPTER 7

EXCELLENCE

"Excellence is the unlimited ability to improve the quality of what you have to offer." | Rick Pitino, basketball coach

Too often, people hold themselves back because they lack the confidence to try something new or take a risk. They dim their own light and make themselves smaller and shrink from their grand potential. We are all capable of excellence when given the tools and concepts to succeed.

Aristotle once said, "We are what we repeatedly do. Excellence, then, is not an act, but a habit." You don't achieve excellence—you continue to strive for it. And every time you think you've achieved it, you need to raise the bar on yourself, or someone else will raise it for you.

Excellence isn't an accident. It's deliberate. It requires focus and commitment, and it begins with setting the standard for yourself that you are a person who embodies excellence. It is who you are. Once you commit to that standard, and make it both your intention and an expectation for yourself, you can move on to addressing the following key elements of excellence one by one:

- Focus

- How you do anything is how you do everything (pay attention to the details)

- Do it now, and do it well

- Go the extra mile

- Continuously improve

FOCUS

What "practice, practice, practice" is to hard work, "focus, focus, focus" is to excellence. When it comes to hard work, focus is critical for excellence. Excellence *requires* focus.

Just as a light bulb will scatter the rays to light an entire room, if you take those same beams of light and focus them into a laser, it will cut through steel. Both are light—but when focused, the immense power of a simple beam of light is nothing short of unimaginable.

This is true for humans, as well: the more you focus, the more precise and powerful your abilities will become.

But what should you focus on?

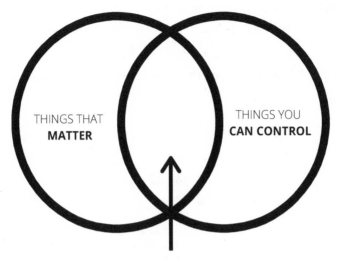

WHAT TO **FOCUS ON**

This graphic illustrates an important point: first and foremost, and as a general rule, your focus needs to sit in the overlap between things that matter and things you can control.

A great question to start or end each day with is, "If I could only accomplish one thing today/tomorrow, what would get me closer to my key objectives or goals?"

You might come up with more than one thing, and if you do—write them all down and put them in order from most important to least important (but make sure you have no more than five things on your list).

Legend has it that Charles Schwab, founder of Bethlehem Steel Corporation, hired a man named Ivy Lee as a productivity consultant in the early 1900s to help him maximize his productivity, both personally and for the company. As the story goes, Lee gave Schwab a technique that he said would cost him nothing unless it worked. "After three months," he said, "you can send me a check for whatever you feel it's worth to you." Lee's simple method for achieving peak productivity had only five steps:

1. At the end of each workday, write down the six most important things you need to accomplish tomorrow. Do not write down more than six tasks.

2. Prioritize those six items in order of their true importance.

3. When you arrive tomorrow, concentrate only on the first task. Work until the first task is finished before moving on to the second task.

4. Approach the rest of your list in the same fashion. At the end of the day, move any unfinished items to a new list of six tasks for the following day.

5. Repeat this process every working day.

Three months later, Schwab ended up paying him $25,000 (which is equivalent to almost half a million dollars in today's value) because of the dramatic effect this technique had on his company's productivity.[4]

Between the overlap of the things that matter and the things you can control, and focusing only on the most important thing first until it's done, you'll be working hard AND smart and the results will be obvious by your successes.

HOW YOU DO ANYTHING IS HOW YOU DO EVERYTHING

My dad's own daily to-do list was always written on the same type of paper—a single sheet from a yellow legal pad. He kept it in the same spot every day, and he didn't just write a daily to-do list for himself—he wrote one for each of his four kids every morning, too. He left them on the kitchen table for us—I never saw him write a to-do list for my mom though, which may explain their fifty-plus year marriage.

Even though the to-do list he wrote out for each of his four kids was different every day, and the chores were all different from each other, the tidiness of his printing was always the same. Remember, he was a military guy, so it always looked the same and it was always in perfect penmanship. Now when I have to fill out a form, people remark that I print like an engineer. That's the way I grew up. "If you're going to write something,

---

4   Rich Bellis, "This 100-Year-Old To-Do List Hack Still Works Like A Charm," Fast Company (Fast Company, August 24, 2016), https://www.fastcompany.com/3062946/this-100-year-old-to-do-list-hack-still-works-like-a-charm.

do it correctly," was his philosophy. "Be intentional. Don't make it sloppy; if you do, it's a reflection of you."

He was right—paying attention to the details in business and in life is another important hallmark of excellence.

Following a recent presentation I did, the boss of the company commented that she was really impressed with the way I communicate and the way I don't use very many non-words. I responded to her that that's incredibly intentional. I work really hard at it. Years ago, I attended a communications program that my company put their frontline managers through; it was one of those foundation-building programs. We each took turns presenting, and then (like a football video analysis) we would watch our film and the other attendees gave us constructive criticism. We would get feedback about how we were communicating with our body language, how we were communicating verbally, and the use of what they called non-words. It was tough criticism to hear at the time, but it is something that has stuck with me all these years later. It's why I practice so thoroughly for the Q&A part of an earnings call—I want to instill confidence in investors. And using words like, "um," "uh," and, "you know," says you aren't able to be concise in your thinking and your communication. And just like my dad used to say, if you can't even do that well, why would I trust that you can go out and execute on something else?

How you present yourself, whether physically, in writing, or in the way you communicate, creates an impression about you. (I'll note that the exception seems to be doctors and surgeons, who—for decades—have been known to be precise, yet also have notoriously bad handwriting. They seem to get a societal pass on being judged on their penmanship—perhaps because they're typically so good at what they do? That may be another side benefit of excellence—a higher forgiveness factor for your shortcomings when the value you provide is so significant?)

If you're going to take the time to do the little things right, there's a good chance I can trust you're going to do the big things with an equal level of capability. If you're sloppy over here, you're probably going to be sloppy elsewhere. If you're precise over here, there's a good chance you're probably going to be precise elsewhere and I can trust that you're a precise person.

WHATEVER YOU DO, DO IT THOROUGHLY.

The idioms, "God is in the detail," and its counterpart, "the devil is in the detail," have been attributed to a number of individuals dating as far back as the 1820s. Regardless of the original source, or which phrase you choose, the general idea is that whatever one does should be done thoroughly.

An example of one such detail I'm fanatical about is email subject lines.

You might laugh and think it's absurd initially, but hear me out.

How many times have you received an email with a blank subject line, or the subject line "Re:"? To me, an email with that subject means that there *is* no subject matter. And to make a point, I've occasionally ignored those emails. And then, when the person says in conversation, "Oh, hey, I sent you an email and I don't think you responded to it." I'll ask, "Oh, when was that?" And then I'll go into my email while I'm on the phone with them and say, "Oh, that one. I didn't know what that was. There was nothing in the subject line," just to make the point that if you don't let people know that some action is required, you're forcing them to go into every single email. And if you force people to do that every time, pretty soon they're going to stop. Or at least that's my experience.

I was recently having an email exchange with a very, very high ranking government official about my company's ability to scale up our test manufacturing. My ask was for support (money) from the US government, so we could scale up our testing to help critically-ill hospitalized patients have a better outcome. At T2 Biosystems, we exist to treat critically-ill hospitalized patients so that they don't die from sepsis. I wanted him to know what our capabilities were, and to be clear to him what this was about, so the subject line of our email thread was T2 Biosystems/COVID-19 Manufacturing Expansion. At a certain point in the email chain, he changed the topic but didn't change the email subject line. He switched gears and was now asking if there was any reason to believe that our technology could be advantageous to test for another disease type. Interestingly enough, we had already developed what we believed was a great test for that disease—and I was able to respond with data that shows ours is actually more sensitive than what's out there in the market. I responded to him with all of this almost immediately, and I intentionally changed the subject line because I knew he would likely forward the email to others. I didn't want him to forward a message of mine with COVID-19 in the subject line, because at the time everybody was getting a million COVID-19 emails and this was different and more specific. Sure enough, he said, "This is awesome, John, I'm forwarding your response to several of my colleagues." Perfect. So—if I hadn't changed that subject line, what they'd think they were getting was another email about COVID-19. Sure, they would see it was from a government official, but he's probably sending them a lot of stuff. Now they know exactly what they're getting, and they were more likely to open it. To me this is just one small example of being intentional about how you communicate with people. It's not just about what you're actually going to say that matters, but the small (or in my opinion, not so small) details of how you frame what you're going to say—which includes your email subject line.

In the same way that even your handwriting is designed to instill confidence in you from the other person, this example not only showcases the importance of clarity in communication but—perhaps, even more importantly—the idea of sharing with intention that the other party is going to forward that email on. By thinking this way you're not only setting things in motion, but you're also preparing for others to receive that forward and know exactly what to do with it because it was intentionally designed with that level of clarity. To many people it might seem like "just a subject line," but to me—if that's their position, they're missing the intentionality and the ten layers that are embedded within that one decision altogether and how powerful that level of attention to detail can be.

DO IT NOW, AND DO IT WELL

One Saturday morning, I went downstairs and I saw the lists of chores my dad had left on the kitchen table for each of us to do. As in business, or in sports, the person who is deemed the "workhorse" in the group generally gets most of the work—and among my siblings, that was usually me. Or at least I thought so. My list ran the entire page. I glanced at my siblings' lists, and they weren't quite as long. I tried to object to that, which didn't go over very well with my dad. He told me, "You have a choice. You can do those chores right away and the rest of the day is yours, OR you can put them off until later, and they will hang over your head all day like a dark cloud. The choice is yours, but the chores are not going to get done on their own."

That was an important learning, to not put things off or procrastinate. He was right—the few times I decided to let the list sit there and didn't do my chores right away were powerful lessons in the truth of his wisdom. It felt so awful to me that I rarely did it again.

I took a page out of his yellow pad 'book', so to speak, and now I have my own mantra for my own sons: *Do it now, and do it well.*

GO THE EXTRA MILE (DO MORE THAN IS EXPECTED)

If you've ever been in a hospital for more than an hour, you realize very quickly the nurses actually run the hospital. They make it work, and they save the patients' lives. Yes, surgeons and doctors come in and out and do what they do—with excellence—but the nurses are the ones caring for the patients twenty-four seven. I had a nurse practitioner who would stay with me after her shift and sit by my bedside and hold the hand of my frail, forty-poundslighter-body and say, "You've got this. We're here for you. We're going to fight this with you." My nurses didn't need to do that. *She* certainly didn't need to do that. She had a life outside the hospital, she had a family of her own, and she had just worked a twelve-hour shift. That, to me, is the definition of going above and beyond the call of duty. But it's going the extra mile that is the ultimate differentiator and truly changes the game for you and everyone around you.

I look at what she was doing—which was way beyond her job responsibilities as a nurse—as being a leader. When things are going perfectly, a leader's job is to validate how great things are. The job of a leader when you're in crisis, however, is to inspire or to instill hope in people. And I think what she was doing in her own way was trying to give me hope, which is a really important responsibility for leaders. I think people sometimes look at leadership as though it belongs on an organizational chart, only those in management, but the truth is, leadership has nothing to do with rank. It's a way of being. And if you show up as a leader, you will inevitably rise within an organization and find yourself in the position on the org chart you once thought belonged to someone other than you.

When you're stretched to capacity with the number of patients you need to see and the number of lives you're trying to save, it's probably easier to just do your job. But doing more than your responsibility and going the extra mile while doing that job is where all the magic is. It's the difference between saving lives and changing lives. It's the definition of true excellence.

CONSTANT IMPROVEMENT

Author and speaker Brian Tracy says, "Excellence is not a destination; it's a continuous journey that never ends."

Trying to be even one percent better tomorrow than you were today, and to be one percent better today than you were yesterday is a concept I love, because it's all about constant improvement.

Whether you call it "kaizen" (the Japanese term for continuous improvement) or "the slight edge," like the book by the same name, or even Aesop's age-old fable of *The Tortoise and The Hare*—the simplicity of focusing on small incremental improvements or changes in the direction of your goals with consistency can have truly powerful results.

If excellence is a journey, you have to have some kind of feedback loop. That's why I record myself over and over again when I'm practicing for quarterly earnings reports. I want to make sure I'm emphasizing the right words. I want to make sure if I'm trying to be serious, that it's serious. If I'm trying to be inspirational, it's inspirational. The only way to do that is to listen to yourself. And if you want to get it right, and if you want to aim for excellence, you have to practice it in order to continually improve.

Remember, small hinges swing big doors. When you focus, do it now (and do it well), go the extra mile, and commit to constant improvement, before long your name becomes synonymous with excellence. And you'll be well on your way to becoming the world-class leader you are meant to be—regardless of title.

CHAPTER 8

ATTITUDE

"Whether you think you can, or you think you can't—you're right" | Henry Ford

Attitude is everything. People say that all the time, but it's absolutely true.

Even before all this happened, people would see me training—running, cycling, lifting weights, doing P90X—and they'd wonder if I was training for a marathon or a triathlon. They'd always ask me, "What are you training for?" And my answer would always be the same, with a smile. "Life."

Little did I know how important that philosophy would ultimately become.

There are few certainties in life. I am absolutely certain about one thing, and many doctors concurred—if I wasn't in the physical shape I was prior to my ordeal, I wouldn't be here.

But there's something far more important to the successful outcome of my journey than being in good condition physically: *attitude.*

I've always had a good attitude, but I never really used to think much about it. I knew whether in business, or life, it has never failed me to choose a positive outlook. But when it came to saving my life, it was my attitude that was the key differentiator because I refused to quit. I refused to give up.

I was working at a large company who hired a motivational speaker to address our team at a national sales meeting. He started his talk by discussing the notion that attitude is contagious. He said, when people ask you how you are every morning, they don't really want to know how you are. They're just making small talk. He said, "When people ask me, I always respond with a word like *tremendous.* In fact, when you call your significant other tonight from this lovely place in Arizona, and they ask how the meeting is going, say, 'Tremendous!' I guarantee you'll get a reaction."

I remember being back at our headquarters a few days later, and my work area happened to be near the company's CEO. He walked by me that morning and when he asked, "How are you doing, John?" I said, "Tremendous!" He literally took a couple of steps back and said, "Whoa, it must have been a good weekend!" I made a decision to intentionally choose a powerful word from that day onwards.

It's amazing when you start your day like that. When I walk into the office, or I go to a restaurant or a store, and someone asks me how I'm doing, I respond with "Fantastic!" or "Awesome." Why? Because attitude is contagious. And while to some it's "just a word" and a smile, to me it's a very big deal. It makes a difference. You can literally see people's reaction and watch their demeanor change—the impact is immediate.

IT'S A CHOICE

> **"THE GREATEST DISCOVERY OF ALL TIME IS THAT A PERSON CAN CHANGE HIS OR HER FUTURE BY MERELY CHANGING HIS OR HER ATTITUDE."**
> **-OPRAH WINFREY-**

What happens to you in life is one thing, but *who you choose to become as a result of what happens to you* is what tells the real story.

When it comes to attitude, you do have a choice. And if you choose to have a good attitude or a positive outlook, it *can* change your future.

The coolest thing about life is you can choose your attitude EVERY. SINGLE. DAY. If you don't like the one you had yesterday, you can choose a different one today, and then choose again the next day.

The good news is: it's habit forming. If you choose a positive attitude on Monday, Tuesday, Wednesday and Thursday, there's a good chance it won't be long before you're waking up on Friday mornings with a naturally positive attitude. The more you flex the muscle, the more it responds, and the stronger it gets.

When I arrived at Spaulding Rehabilitation Hospital, I entered the state-of-the-art training room on my second day—in a wheelchair. My legs weren't working at all, and I sat there trying to visualize how I was going to get from my current state to walking. There was a guy next to me on the stretching tables. He looked incredibly fit—he was on his back doing crunches and his abs were just shredded. Turns out, he's a double amputee and he was there rehabbing after losing both of his legs. I don't know how or what happened, but this guy's attitude was incredible, and he was laughing and joking with the staff about being physically fit. I literally thought to myself, *I don't care how tough this is. Whatever I went through or whatever I still might have to go through, somebody always has it tougher than me.*

On day four, a guy came into the rehab room in a military issue wheelchair with his name (Vincent) on the side. I later learned they had been clearing out buildings during Operation Enduring Freedom and he and a few other guys went to go into a building and when they kicked open the door, the building exploded.

I don't know the extent of all of his injuries. He was there to rehab from his fortieth surgery, where they had put steel rods in every single one of his toes, on both feet, because they had curled from strokes that he had while he was in a medically-induced coma for more than a year. The explosion took half his head apart, and took one of his limbs completely off. He had suffered significant head trauma so his communication wasn't sharp, and his mobility was obviously limited, but this guy's attitude was remarkable. He was the embodiment of the rehab center's motto, "Find your strength."

After my second week at Spaulding Rehab, I got a call from the wife of one of my best friends. She said, "Steve is on his way to Spaulding." A little perplexed as to why she was calling to tell me that, I responded, "Great, I can't wait to see him." She went on to tell me that he had a stroke and he was being admitted for rehab. Can you imagine, one of my best friends, my running partner for over ten years, was admitted to Spaulding at the same time as me? What are the odds of that?

Those are only a few of so many examples of the incredible people I saw and met during my month at Spaulding. Even in the worst circumstances, those guys chose to continue smiling and approached each challenge with a positive attitude. And it made a difference. To them—and to me.

While I was there, I caught the immense positivity from everyone around me—and I'm already a guy who wakes up not needing anyone to raise the positivity level on his attitude. But it did. It was incredibly motivating, and had an enormous impact on me, my recovery, and who I am today.

HOW ATTITUDE AFFECTS OUTCOMES

My time at Spaulding helped drive home the point for me, and hopefully for you, that the attitude you choose is critically important—and if you choose a positive attitude it can really create a positive outcome. In life, in business, in sports—attitude is your most important survival skill. In my case, it literally helped to save my life.

Attitude affects how you communicate and how you collaborate with others. And this one's really important: the attitude you bring to your work, your home, and your group of friends impacts the culture. As a CEO, I spend a lot of time focusing on strategy and culture, and I want to underscore how each and every person affects the culture of a work environment. The Chairman and CEO of Baxter, a multi-billion dollar global healthcare company, wrote a really insightful piece on strategy and culture, and how critical culture is to the success of their company. He went as far as to say that, "Culture eats strategy for breakfast. And for lunch and dinner, too."

The fact that attitude is contagious can also be the worst part about it. It's a double-edged sword. If you come home from work and have a bad attitude, it affects your friends and family. If you walk into work and have an awesome attitude, it affects everyone around you. The people around you are either lifted up—or pulled down—by your attitude. It can suck the energy out of a room, or brighten it entirely. With choice comes great responsibility, and as a result of an interview with Jill Bolte Taylor that gave her one of her greatest a-ha moments on air, Oprah now has a sign adorning her makeup room which reads, "Please take responsibility for the energy you bring into this space."

Taking ownership of *your* space, or taking responsibility for your own physical wellbeing is connected to being mentally fit. And being mentally fit is connected to your energy. Your energy is connected to your attitude. And your attitude is connected to having confidence and control in your life.

Whether you like them or not, Peyton Manning, Tom Brady and Drew Brees are three of the best quarterbacks to have ever played in the National Football League. Not surprisingly, they rank one, two and three in fourth-quarter comebacks for their teams. Each one of them has done this more than thirty times in his career. It's unprecedented. When they enter the huddle in the fourth quarter, with the game on the line, do you think they say, "Look, guys, it's the fourth quarter, and we're behind, so let's try to score," OR do you think they say, "Guys, we're going to drive the ball down the field one play at a time and we're going to win this game"? I'm pretty sure they walk into that huddle and the attitude they display is one of complete positivity. In their minds, the game is already won. It sets the direction for the rest of the team and it drives a much more positive outcome—the results speak for themselves.

PLAY TO WIN

Years ago, I organized a national sales meeting and the theme was based on a samurai warrior called Miyamoto Musashi, who won more than sixty death duels, and wrote *The Book of Five Rings.* The theme of our meeting was, "The Way of Excellence"—the way of a warrior.

Musashi said that warriors have a purpose—to fight—and the reason they fight is to win.

If, like a warrior, the reason you play the game—your purpose—is to win, you need to focus your attention on what you want and then go for it. If your intention is set on winning, you're much more likely to be successful because you're willing to *prepare* to win.

Consider a youth soccer game where the parents don't put the score on display because they don't want little Joey to see that his team lost. Whether it's posted for all to see or not, the kids still know the score. *We all do.*

In competition, in any place we "keep score"—whether on the sports scoreboard or through the KPIs and metrics in our business—it's human nature to want to win. If you're not keeping score, then it's a hobby. You don't have to play to win when it's a hobby. But if there's a scoreboard, and if the person or the team with the most points wins, then let's decide—let's make a bold, intentional choice—*to play to win.*

STAY HUMBLE

When I was twenty-eight years old and one of the youngest vice presidents in a large global company, I was fortunate to work for a guy we all called Mac. Besides being a great guy, he was an outstanding mentor—and he took that role seriously.

When I think back to people that worked for him, many went on to become presidents and CEOs. When it was obvious I was getting a little overconfident, he gave me an incredibly valuable life lesson in something I learned would be critical to my success: humility.

He sat me down and said, "I think you're really good, John. *Everybody* thinks you're really good. But it's important to stay humble.

"I want you to do an experiment when you get home tonight. Go to your garage and get a bucket—a good sized bucket that you might wash your car with—fill it up with water, and put it on the floor. Then put your hand inside the water, down to your wrist, and then pull your hand out really fast and see what kind of impression it leaves."

"I don't need to do the experiment," I said. "I get the message, and it's an important one. Thank you. Though I might have an impact while my hand is in the bucket, and while the composition of the water might be different after I leave, it does go back to its original form almost instantly."

Sometimes it's hard to hear, but it's true—everyone is replaceable, and it's important to stay humble no matter what.

AN ATTITUDE OF GRATITUDE

When I was in the hospital, the nurses and doctors were in and out of my room twenty four hours a day and they were constantly asking how I felt. My answer was always the same, because it *is* always the same. I choose the same words all the time. It's either great, fantastic, terrific or awesome. Can you imagine the look on the nurses' and doctors' faces when this guy who needs a heart transplant, who is lying in the ICU and fighting for his life responds, "I'm great" or "I'm awesome"? They know this patient is one of the sickest people in a hospital with more than a thousand beds. And that person is saying they're great or they're awesome.

I said, "I'm great" or "I'm awesome" because—the truth is—I was. And I *am*. I'm ALIVE!

I was awake and able to think and able to breathe and able to speak.

And for that, I was truly grateful.

Not believing me, they'd ask me more direct questions about my pain level. They'd say, "OK, 'awesome' John, on a scale of one to ten, with ten being the highest, how's your pain?" I would always answer, "Zero." I literally *always* said zero. And I remember one time a nurse saying, "Uh… we just did a sternotomy on you yesterday. You know that operation where they cut your chest open, saw your sternum, and pry your ribs apart? You *can't* be a zero." And I responded, "OK. Fine. It's a one." Sometimes you have to throw people a bone.

And sometimes—even through the darkest of times—you have to laugh and look for any ounce of perspective you can find that will lead to gratitude.

I believe it is so important to embody gratitude, be thankful, and show appreciation for, and with, your colleagues, your customers, and of course, your family.

Every time I go to Mass General Hospital, I still go back up to the floor where I spent a couple of months, even though many of the nurses and doctors are starting to turn over. On the one-year anniversary of my release, Rhonda and my son Kyle and I went and spent the day there, bringing breakfast and lunch and dinner to all of the shifts. It felt like I had a personal connection with every single person. And when I go back now, it feels a little different because I don't know all the nurses and doctors anymore, but it is still so important to me to show up there and in my own way give them hope and inspiration to persevere and continue to give the best of what they have every day—even though it's hard. They work long hours, and most of the patients in the cardiac ICU don't have the same good outcome I had. They appreciate that a patient is willing to come back, even years later, to show his gratitude and be a living example of the great work they're doing. I see it lifting them up firsthand, and—as always seems to be the case with giving—I end up getting way more out of it than they do.

It's because Alex made the decision to become an organ donor that I'm even here today, and I can't help but wake up feeling grateful for him and the decision that literally saved my life. And it's such a privilege to get to pay that forward in the role I have, at the helm of T2 Biosystems, using my talents and the life I've been given to advance life-saving technologies.

Cultivating an attitude of gratitude by living each day with a gratitude practice, and choosing a powerful word to become my positive "attitude anchor" for the day have been two of the most impactful habits I've ever built.

If you buy into the fact that attitudes are indeed contagious, why on earth would you ever choose one that isn't positive?

CHAPTER 9

RESILIENCE

"Strength does not come from physical capacity. It comes from indomitable will." | Mahatma Gandhi

If you look up resilience in the dictionary, it is defined as, "the capacity to recover quickly from difficulties; toughness." In essence, it is our ability to recover from adversity. Whether it's a setback, an illness, a loss, or just sheer pain, resiliency is a critical skill to possess in life.

You can be humming along in life or business or sport or leisure, and then all of a sudden you get completely blindsided. It's how you deal with and respond to the situation that is going to determine your success or not.

I went to the University of Maine at Orono, which—if you played high school football in Maine—you know is the top college football program in the state. My belief was that I was going to be a quarterback at UMaine, but the coach that recruited me left in the summer, and the new head coach had a different offensive philosophy. My skills as a quarterback weren't a good fit, I was moved to the defensive side of the ball, and I ended up playing defensive back in my first year at UMaine.

I think it was probably the best thing that could have happened to me, because it was the first time I had ever had any kind of a setback in sports. I was used to deciding I wanted something and going after it with relentless determination, work my butt off, and get it. This was the first time I experienced something unexpected that was outside of my control. I didn't plan that. And it forced me to ask, *now what? How am I going to react to this?* I knew I had a choice in my response, and I decided to embrace it, play defense, and give it everything I had. And in the end, I got a *lot* stronger. The way you work out as a quarterback is very different than the way you work out as a defensive player. The way you *think* as a quarterback is very different than the way you think as a defensive player.

For my sophomore year I transferred from the University of Maine to Plymouth State College in New Hampshire, which was a division-three college football program. I had to sit out a year before I could play, because I was transferring from a division one school to a division three school. So I went home, and I got two jobs—one of which was as an assistant coach for my brother's high school football team. I sat out the fall, and then I went to Plymouth State that winter. There, I played quarterback for the next three years, and having spent a year thinking as a defensive player and then acting as an assistant coach, I became a *much* better quarterback. I now understood something I never did before—how defense actually thinks about stopping an offense. As a quarterback, I always used to think, *We have a game plan. We go out and execute our game plan. It really doesn't matter what the defensive players do.* But now I had a much better appreciation for the way defensive players thought and the way they're taught to react to different offensive schemes. It made me a better—and certainly more intelligent—quarterback.

When I talked to my college coach recently, he jokingly said, "You weren't the best athlete on the team, but you *were* the hardest working and smartest." I was the strongest quarterback on the team, and I certainly worked hard, but the smarts he was talking about came from my experience with the gift that came hidden inside adversity.

Sometimes we get so wrapped up in the emotion and disappointment of what happens to us when things don't go our way, that we miss the gift entirely. We don't give it our all anymore where we are, and as a result, we miss the chance to become better for the chance that will usually be given to us in the future that we can't yet see.

When I showed up at Plymouth State, I was back to being a quarterback—but in our first game I had to deal with being positioned as the number two guy behind the incumbent, who was really good. He was a year ahead of me, and got the start in the first game we played. Luckily for me, I suppose, he didn't have a good game. Our team lost its first game, which ended a nineteen-game winning streak. And this prompted the coach to change quarterbacks. I started the next game, played very well, and we won in convincing fashion. The other quarterback was relegated to the backup role for the rest of the season.

Fast forward to my junior year—his senior year—and I got sick in preseason. I was so sick I couldn't even get out of bed (and I'm a guy who has to be *really sick* not to go practice). I was so sick I couldn't move. I was literally flat on my back in bed for almost two full weeks and meanwhile, the other quarterback was having a great run, and the guys were saying, "Hey, Larry looks really good." I thought to myself, *It's okay. I'll beat him out.* But I never got the chance. He had a phenomenal year and I became the backup. I know a lot about myself, and I am *not* a good second lieutenant. I don't take to that role easily. It was uncomfortable. But it was something I had to learn. And I really had to learn it. It rocked me at my core to be standing on the sideline, watching this guy, when I felt it should be me. But, if you want to lead, you must learn how to follow.

He had an incredible year, and it was great for the team. And I was part of that team. But I can tell you, I didn't like it *at all*. And that's why, when it came to my senior year, it was going to be *my year*—my team—and I was going to lead that team to accomplish great things. We were primed and ready as we had won several championships... two in my sophomore year—a New England Football Conference Championship and an Eastern Collegiate Athletic Conference championship, the first the team had ever done—and another New England Football Conference championship along with the first trip to the NCAAs the year I had to sit and watch.

ADVERSITY

While attitude is all about choice, adversity is different in the sense that sometimes it just chooses you. Adversity comes in different forms and—like pain—it is a universal concept, but the unique experience of pain is going to be different for each person. One thing is clear about both pain and adversity, try as you might, when it comes looking for you, it's not something you can dodge. In my case, I got diagnosed with giant cell myocarditis, a disorder that has been diagnosed approximately 300 times in medical history, most of those during autopsy. How can you possibly prepare for something like that?

Perhaps one of the greatest lessons I've learned in life is that *it's not what happens to you, it's who you choose to become as a result of what happens to you* that ultimately defines who you are—and dictates the level of success you'll achieve in life.

ADVERSITY DOESN'T BUILD CHARACTER, IT REVEALS IT.

We watch how people behave in a crisis and it's totally different than how they might react in a less stressful situation. And that was clearly the case with me. I was in the lab talking to one of the nurses *after I had survived*, and he said, "What you physically put yourself through was unheard of, but the psychological impact must have been overwhelming. Didn't you just want to lay down and die?" And I said, "I never let it get overwhelming. I refused to allow negative thoughts to enter my brain."

Well, of course negative thoughts *did* try to creep in once in a while (I'm only human), but when they did—I shut them out. When you're there in the hospital, laying on your back for twenty-four hours a day, day after day, week after week, they're going to creep in, but I had to be mentally tough enough to shut them out. Hard work, perseverance and grit are what made me successful in sports. It's what has made me successful in business. And it's what got me through that crisis in the hospital—sheer determination and raw grit and will.

Ultimately, adversity revealed that I'm a fighter beyond even what I believed. It revealed this indomitable will, a will that absolutely saved my life. "The will to live," as they call it, is actually a real thing. People in the hospital told me regularly that it mattered, and now—whenever I am in the hospital and I have the opportunity to visit with patients—the one thing I tell them is that you have to fight and never give up. It's a different kind of fight when you're critically ill and fighting for your life. In business, we often fight to reach our quarterly or annual targets. In sports, we typically fight to outscore our opponent. In each case, there is a finite amount of time. You know that you have a week remaining in the quarter, or two minutes left in the game. But when you're fighting for your life, or fighting AND waiting for a life-saving organ transplant, you don't know how long it will take—or if it will ever come. It is a fight against time for which there is no clock. You have to keep fighting and fighting and fighting. And you don't know if it's a day, a week, a month, or many months. For most people, it's really difficult to sustain that level of fight in the face of so much uncertainty. But when the will to live kicks in, and you are willing to give it everything you have—and I mean *everything*—you can pretty much conquer anything. And knowing it can save your life, just imagine what it can do for you on a day to day basis!

I felt so strongly about putting adversity into this section because without it, I'm actually not doing you justice. When people have an expectation that life is supposed to be easy, they're absolutely taken down to their core when adversity hits. I'd far rather give adversity its fair place in the equation, as part of what triggers you to be living the best possible life that only you can lead.

ONE OF THE GREATEST GIFTS ADVERSITY
CAN GIVE US IS THE HIDDEN GIFT OF
TRUE PURPOSE.

THE THREE STEPS TO RESILIENCE

I've come to believe there are three steps in the process of building resilience:

- ACKNOWLEDGE the reality of the current situation
- ACCEPT uncertainty & confront your fear(s)
- FOCUS on the solution & take action

STEP ONE:
ACKNOWLEDGE THE REALITY OF THE
CURRENT SITUATION

You've read my story of being diagnosed with one of the world's rarest and deadliest disorders, needing a heart transplant, and having almost no chance of survival. I'm very good at acknowledging the reality of a situation. When it came to my medical situation, it was somewhat easy. I knew I was in the fight of my life. I knew I needed a heart transplant. I knew it was going to be a tough battle, physically and mentally. I could easily acknowledge the reality of my situation.

STEP TWO:
ACCEPT UNCERTAINTY & CONFRONT YOUR FEAR(S)

Accepting uncertainty and confronting your fear is the part of the equation that I'm truthfully not the best at. Personally, as it relates to my health journey, I skipped right past this step. I wasn't worried about the uncertainty. I wasn't worried about fear. I had a positive attitude and I was determined to survive. My will to live overrode the process, and I simply didn't allow any negativity, or doubt, to enter my mind. You'd be surprised how hard you're willing to fight when your life is really and truly—I mean, *literally*—on the line.

I recognize this was an extreme example, but even in non-life-or-death situations I tend to skip right by this stage, and—as a leader—this is something I have to be very aware of. People move through different stages at different paces. Because I'm not good at showing, or even feeling fear—sometimes when it's not part of the equation from my perspective, I don't remember to take time to acknowledge that those around me might be scared and might need support, even if I don't feel that way. I tend to move straight into step three, and assume others are right there with me, which can come across to my team and my family as a little cold and impersonal.

I did a color wheel personality profile test a while back, and it spoke to this area directly: "You naturally think through your options before taking a position. And when you take a position, you tend to be decisive and direct with an informal down-to-earth communication style. You may be inclined to address others in concrete terms, without regard for their feelings. It's for this reason you're quite often the one who is called upon to make the tough calls and make sure people comply." I think that's so dead on. Rhonda tells me that sometimes, in a crisis, it seems like I don't care about people's feelings. I know that. And it's not because I don't care about them—to me, it's just better not to confuse the facts with emotion. And in relationships, that's admittedly not always the best way, but in terms of solving a crisis, it's very effective. Now, when I find myself in this type of situation, I'm working on saying, before I move into decisive action, "This is a crisis. We need to act fast. Feelings might get hurt along the way when we're in action mode, and I might not notice because I am so focused on the solution. But what I can promise, is that when the crisis is over, we'll debrief, talk about how everyone felt, and go through any collateral damage that may have inadvertently and unintentionally happened in the haste of getting us out of crisis mode. Even stopping long enough to utilize this sound byte has been a learning process for me, and doesn't come all that naturally.

STEP THREE:
FOCUS ON THE SOLUTION & TAKE ACTION

I didn't know exactly what my path toward survival would entail but I knew that staying totally focused—I'm talking *laser* focused—could be the difference between living and dying.

The global COVID-19 pandemic was an unbelievable exercise in resilience for so many people. At my company, we had to acknowledge the reality of our situation—our sales people could no longer enter hospitals, and our service/support people could only enter hospitals to provide emergency equipment service or repairs. We had to accept the uncertainty and confront our fears presented by the unknown. And then we had to move into action and focus on a solution. The realities of our situation forced us to rethink well-established ways of doing business and required us to find really creative ways to support our existing customers—and win new ones. Members of our sales team are now taking customers all the way from an introductory phone call to selling them an instrument that costs tens of thousands of dollars by video conference. And then having to send someone in to install the equipment in a matter of weeks, versus what often took months before, because our customers are also in unprecedented circumstances. They're also dealing with tremendous uncertainty, and as a result they're actually willing to do things that they might not have ever done. And it's working. It's a win-win for everyone.

WE ALL NEED REMINDERS

I wear this blue silicone bracelet on my wrist, one of those free promotional swag items they hand out at conferences (you know the kind, like the LIVESTRONG bracelet Lance Armstrong made famous). This particular one was from the vice president of an investment bank, who handed me a couple of bags of them when I arrived and casually said, "Oh, by the way, I had something made and we're giving them out today." For the people at the conference who knew my story, they thought it rocked, and for those who didn't they asked a lot of questions. Although I know him very well, I didn't ask him to make the bracelets, he just did so of his own accord. It read NEVER GIVE UP.

The year after my heart transplant, Rhonda and I were in Hawaii and we decided to hike a dormant volcano called Koko Head Crater. It's not a huge volcano, but it's super steep. Because of that, climbing it is considered the glute workout from hell. While I don't know exactly how high it is, I certainly can attest to the fact that everyone agrees it's a good thing when you're done and you find yourself thinking *Thank God I'm finished with that* when it's over. It has an old military railroad track that goes straight up, and the railroad ties are a little bit of a stretch to go from one to the other, even for really fit people. In my prime, I probably would have run up Koko Head, but when I couldn't feel my legs from the knees down and I was still recovering from a heart transplant, I wasn't about to try running up this StairMaster from hell. I wasn't in top shape at the time, and halfway up I found myself feeling tired and thinking that this might actually be a little more than I bargained for. It was tougher than I thought, and at the halfway point I started thinking to myself, *I've got a pretty good view from here and it might be too risky to keep climbing. Maybe I'll just turn around and enjoy the view and hike back down.* And on this day, at just that moment, I happened to look down at my wrist and the writing on my blue bracelet was facing out. The words NEVER GIVE UP were practically shouting at me from my wrist. It gave me the extra push I needed to forge on, and when I got to the top I was so glad I made it, because the view from the top was *way* better than the one from halfway up.

I wear that bracelet every day as a reminder that no matter what the odds, and no matter how bleak things look, you can't quit. And the concept of never giving up is an important message for everyone. Sometimes we all need a little reminder.

CHAPTER 10

TEAMWORK

"It is teamwork that remains the ultimate competitive advantage, both because it is so powerful and rare." | Patrick Lencioni

While the first four parts of the HEART acronym are more related to self, the last piece of the puzzle is about others. It's about how you work as a team, how you build a solid culture that attracts the best people, and how to come together to create success.

TEAMWORK MAKES THE DREAM WORK

For a team to work, they have to want it. They have to have a common interest, a common cause. They must focus on—and advance toward—their desired results. Effective and amazing teams have great leadership, and they communicate well—honestly, and openly. The best teams I've seen play off each other's strengths.

The worst teams I've seen aren't really teams at all. More often than not, they're groups of selfish individuals. And it doesn't need to be a large group of selfish players to ruin a team; just a single bad apple can spoil the bunch, as the saying goes.

In hockey, there are those players who don't make the pass, even when they see it and ultimately they should. Even just a second's hesitation matters. Even if the player decides to make that pass a second later, the opportunity is gone. The window is closed, and inside that hesitation was inherent selfishness. They weren't thinking of being a playmaker— they were thinking of making that extra move to beat the player in front of them, or perhaps being the goal scorer.

What they fail to realize is that they're actually likely to score a lot more often when their goal is to become a playmaker. They're much more likely to make the *right* play instead of the play they think is going to lead to the outcome they want.

I learned a long time ago the best thing you can do as a leader is to surround yourself with great people—people who are playmakers. Effective CEOs have to be able to identify talent and cultivate it. I believe it is my responsibility— and one of the most important things I do as a leader—to develop people.

NOT JUST ANY PEOPLE, YOU NEED THE *RIGHT* PEOPLE

As a leader, I want to be known as the guy who galvanizes a bunch of really, really smart people. I want to bring together people who are all brighter and more talented than I am. Then, it becomes my job as the leader to get those brilliant people to move around a common vision, mission or set of objectives.

But as a leader, it also goes beyond just surrounding yourself with the best—you have to listen to what they have to say, respect it, and act on it.

And as Jim Collins explains in his landmark business book *Good to Great*, it's not just about having the right people on the right bus—you also need to have the right people in the right seats.

In football, there are a few different buses—there's an offensive bus, a defensive bus, and a special teams bus. Offense is scripted; you go into the huddle, the quarterback calls the play, and you go execute. Of course, sometimes you change the play at the line of scrimmage, but you know you're going to run a specific, well-rehearsed play. Defense, however, doesn't know exactly what play the offense will run and, while they prepare based on down-and-distance and other tendencies, they're generally reacting to what the opponent does.

My college football coach was a college quarterback himself in his younger days. I thought that meant he would be very offensive-minded, and he generally was. But he would often say—which I'll admit I didn't like one bit, given that I was an offensive player—"You're all good athletes, but you have to be a better athlete to play defense because they don't know what's coming. I put my best athletes on defense; everyone else plays offense." And he was right. You need to have the right people in the right seats, so they can play to each other's strengths.

The same goes in business: the people who are going to help you innovate are often not the same people that are going to help you market and sell to customers. The people that market and sell to customers are not usually the same people you want dealing with customer problems. It takes a different level of empathy and a different set of strengths to be able to do that.

Do you have the right people on your team, and are they in the right positions?

The right people on the team in business must include diversity. Most people immediately associate the general term "diversity" to mean ethnic diversity. But successful teams need diversity of all kinds; ethnic, yes, but is there diversity in age? And gender diversity? They are *all* really important.

Leadership is about ensuring you have the right people and the right culture—and that culture begins and ends with you.

And to me, the most important element of leadership is trust.

TRUST

Knowing someone else has your back is critical in any kind of team environment. At a typical Monday football practice in college, which we called "conditioning day," our coach would have us run laps around the athletic complex at the end of practice. I was a dedicated and determined guy; I didn't drink during the season, and I would stay in peak condition. This meant I would start to lap the other players after a couple of laps around the complex. One Monday we were out for our run and a lot of the guys were just doggin' it after partying all weekend. As I came up to lap a group of my teammates, our coach yelled, "If Sperzel laps even *one* person, everybody gets an extra mile." So I start to slow down because I don't want to stick it to my teammates like that. That prompts the coach to then yell, "Sperzel, if you *don't* lap anybody you get an extra three miles." I took the extra three miles that day. Afterwards, with all my teammates already in the locker room, I asked the coach why he did that. He said it was to see how I would react. I called nonsense, and told him that he already knew how I would react—to which he replied, "Yeah, but I wanted your teammates to see it."

Simon Sinek, author of *Start With Why*, posted a great video on Facebook[5] entitled "Performance vs. Trust." In the video he explains how when he worked with the Navy Seals he asked them how they pick who goes onto Seal Team Six (they are the best of the best of the best of the best). He said they drew a graph for him and on one side they wrote the word Performance. And on the other side, they wrote the

---

5   Simon Sinek, "Performance vs. Trust," Facebook Watch, accessed January 25, 2021, https://www.facebook.com/watch/?v=622314895238946.

word Trust. Performance meant a person's performance on the battlefield and trust meant their performance off the battlefield. In business, performance is your skills. Did you make your quarterly earnings, etc. Traditional performance. Trust, on the other hand, is how you are off the battlefield. What kind of person you are. The way they put it is, "I may trust you with my life, but do I trust you with my money and my wife?"

He said they went on to tell him that nobody wants the person in the bottom left quadrant—the low performer with low trust. And he said, of course, everybody wants the person in the top right hand quadrant—the high performer with high trust. What they learned, however, is that the person in the top left quadrant—the high performer with low trust is a toxic leader and a toxic team member. And they would rather have a medium performer with high trust, or sometimes even a *low* performer with high trust. Remember, he said, this is the highest-performing organization on the planet. And the low performing/high trust person is more important than the high performing/low trust person. "The problem in business," he said, "is we have lopsided metrics. We have a million and one metrics to measure someone's performance and negligible to no metrics to measure someone's trustworthiness. And so what we end up doing is promoting or bonusing toxicity in our businesses, which is bad for the long game because it eventually destroys the whole organization.

"The irony is," he went on to say, "it's unbelievably easy to find these people. Go to any team and say, 'Who's the a**hole?'

and they'll all point to the same person. Equally, if you go to any team and say, "Who do you trust more than anybody else? Who's always got your back and when the chips are down, you know they will be there with you?" They will also all point to the same person. It's the best gifted, natural leader who's creating an environment for everybody else to succeed. They may not be your most individual highest performer, but that person—you better keep them on your team."

ADDITION BY SUBTRACTION

Even if they're a high performer, having a selfish person on the squad is a cancer in a company or on a team. In Boston, the Celtics had a player named Kyrie Irving, who was one of the best basketball players in the NBA but who had a reputation of being a very selfish player. Headlines have followed his career like, "Kyrie Irving's selfish style leads to questions of his ability to lead," and "Former Cavs Coach Slams Kyrie Irving for being a Selfish Teammate." When he left the Boston Celtics, they got better. This is what I call *addition by subtraction*. You get rid of a bad teammate, even if they're a *great* individual player, and the team gets better. Sometimes even exponentially better. I've seen that happen over and over again.

Just as it does when you subtract a team member, every new addition can also impact the culture of the team. Heck, every addition can impact the culture of the *entire organization*. And the impact is magnified on a small team or in a small company. Sometimes where I made mistakes, especially early in my career, was with people—bringing a person onto the team that negatively affected the culture, or knowing that someone had a lot of things they contributed to the company, but not being decisive enough to make that change if they were a culture killer.

I've learned that if you're the leader of a team with a selfish or non-team player and you do nothing, you've just undermined your own leadership ability, which ultimately affects whether or not people will follow you. It might be difficult to do, but as a leader, you simply can't tolerate people that are going to disrupt the team. If you do, the team loses, and so do you. *People are your culture.* Ensuring we have the right people on the team, with the right attitude, is critical to culture development—and EVERYTHING.

DO YOUR JOB

Bill Belichick, the coach of the New England Patriots, has a powerful go-to phrase:—*do your job*. If every person on the team does their job, the team is much more likely to be successful. If you start worrying about the people around you—he didn't do his job, or she could have done a better job—it impacts your ability to do your own job. This is partly because you've taken your focus off what you need to do, lessening your performance, and partly in the destruction of culture that comes from the erosion of trust through criticism and negativity—even in one's thoughts—within the team.

The quote that leads off this chapter on teamwork is by Patrick Lencioni, author of *The Five Dysfunctions of a Team*—a must-read book on creating high performance teams. It's written as a fable, and is a really easy read and/or a quick listen. In the book, one of the key concepts is that great teams are willing to confront issues head on and have healthy conflict. They're willing to call people out who are not doing their job, and they're willing to call people out who are not trusting others. While it may seem counterintuitive that confronting issues head on and having healthy conflict promotes trust, it does. Not verbalizing these things out loud and instead either thinking or talking about them behind people's back is what creates a lack of trust.

Successful teams, and players, need to have well-defined roles and responsibilities. Think of sports where you know that a defenseman has a certain role on a hockey team, or a wide receiver has a certain role on a football team. In business, however, sometimes we just *assume* that people know what their role is on the team. And we all know when you assume things, it rarely ends well. Sometimes it's because of a lack of leadership, and sometimes it's poor communication. Other times it's the wrong players on the team, or the right player in the wrong seat. Taking the time to provide clarity is invaluable in terms of improving a team's performance; outlining and clarifying roles, definitions, responsibilities, deliverables, and outcomes can have a profound impact on an organization. If you want people to perform at the highest level, invest the time to make sure nothing within a person's role is left up to assumption. That way, whether as a coach, leader or fellow player, you can let go and let people do their job.

When I was admitted to the hospital, I had to have full trust that the people around me knew what to do and that they would do their job to save my life. When you enter the hospital as a patient, you check both your dignity and your need to contribute at the door. The only thing I could contribute was a positive attitude and the will to live. Everything else was completely out of my control. I had to trust that the team around me would fight to save my life, and I had to trust that they knew what they needed to do in order to accomplish that—that they knew full well their role and responsibilities. And after that, there was only one thing left for them to do—do your job. If everybody has a purpose and a role on the team, and everybody does their job, then collectively we'll be more likely to be successful—together and individually—both on and off the field.

INTEGRITY

When the chief science officer at my company (a brilliant PhD who was the company's first employee) announced he was leaving to join another start up company, he took me aside and thanked me for showing him what integrity means as a leader. I said, "It's actually very easy to have integrity. My foundation is telling the truth—good, bad, or otherwise—because I will always remember what I said."

By definition, integrity means "the quality of being honest and having strong moral principles; moral uprightness," or "the state of being whole and undivided."

To me, both the quality of being honest and the state of being whole and undivided comes from telling the truth. There's no division with the truth. I never have to think how to answer when somebody asks me a question—I know how to answer it, because I just answer with what is true. Sure, as the CEO of a public company, there are times when I have to say to someone, "I can't answer that question because it's something I can't disclose—it's confidential, and not public information." But if I answer a question directly, I always know how I answered it. There's nothing to try to remember. And if somebody comes back to me, which investors are really good at doing, and says, "By the way, John, on the last earnings call, you said this," I say, "I didn't say that." "No, I'm pretty sure you did." "I'm *certain* that I didn't, because I would remember it." If I start waffling and start going into gray zones, I'll have no idea what I said. And nobody's smart enough to remember all of that. My parents taught me very early: tell the truth, and you'll always remember what you said.

A potential investor recently asked me for certain non-public information, and I said, "We are a public company and that is non-public information, so I'm not going to share it." Even though we're under a nondisclosure agreement, if I did it for them I would need to do it for all other potential investors— otherwise it would be an uneven playing field. I don't work that way. And I told him that. And he said, "Well, other CEOs do it." And I said, "I don't set my moral compass based on what other CEOs do. I set my moral compass myself."

Your integrity must be defined. And then, when you know where the boundaries are, don't compromise on them. Ever. Don't try to take shortcuts to get there—because there aren't any. And if there are, or appears as thought there might be, they're short lived.

When you face a challenge, it's actually the best opportunity to demonstrate professionalism, integrity, and excellence. Sometimes it's hard to spot when everything's going great, but when you're in crisis mode, that's when it really shows up and it really stands out.

If I said to the guy, "Hey, look—wink, wink—I'm going to give you the information, but I'm not *supposed* to give it to you," on some level the guy is never going to trust me again, even if he likes what I said, because deep down he knows I'm willing to break the rules. On the other hand, he might not like it, and he might not invest in the company when I say I'm not going to do it, but he immediately knows I have integrity. There is a respect that comes with integrity that exceeds and outweighs any short-term "deal." Integrity is a pass/fail test: you either have it, or you don't. There is no in between. It takes years to build, and can be gone in an instant. But when you have it—because you've cultivated it and committed to it as a lifelong pursuit—the rewards are priceless and immeasurable, and a team (or player) with integrity is one of the most valuable assets on earth.

But integrity is not just about telling the truth—it's also about standing up for what is right.

STANDING UP FOR WHAT'S RIGHT

I had been a successful salesperson and a successful first line sales manager, so I made the decision to go over to the "dark side"—into marketing.

I had no marketing experience besides sales and my innate ability to lead and understand customers, and as a completely green, very young marketing person I found myself sitting in a meeting where we were talking about hiring an advertising agency. There was this sort of "bake-off" process where three or four agencies competed for the contract; they came in, presented, and then they left and we were to decide.

Our current agency, LehmanMillet, was a marketing communications firm that focused on devices and diagnostics, based in Boston; they were truly the best in the business, and they still remain so even today, although under a different name.

It was obvious to everyone in the room that LehmanMillet was by far the best after the presentations, and given they were the incumbent, everyone already knew the quality of their people and the quality of their work.

Even though it was obvious who was best, the room began gravitating toward a different agency based in Chicago. The company I was working for was based in Indianapolis, and, "Chicago would certainly be easier to get to from Indy—you could just drive three hours straight up the I-65—and this is a high profile pharmaceutical agency, so they probably have all kinds of other accoutrements," they said.

As the conversation played out, I could see where it was heading. We were going to dump this agency who had been there with us from the beginning, and had done an incredible job. For what? Because there was a path that seemed like it was easier, or more convenient. It was just a preference that people had. And they were preparing to change for the sake of change, *not* change because it was the right thing to do for the business.

It was completely wrong.

I stood up.

"Every single person in this room knows that LehmanMillet is the best firm. It's the firm we should be choosing. Why aren't we making that decision?"

The room, and all the people in it, fell absolutely silent.

In the end, the company did decide to forge ahead with LehmanMillet, and it was wildly successful.

When the boss of our division was talking to the founder, he said, "You know, you should go and thank Sperzel, because he really put his neck on the line for you guys."

At that time, I didn't know them at all. I had no relationship with them. I just knew what they had done. And I knew that where we were going wasn't right. And so I just did what I do, which is stand up for what's right.

It's part of integrity, and part of gaining trust, and in my experience—even when it's uncomfortable—standing up for what's right is always the right thing to do.

CONCLUSION

TRUE PURPOSE

"You can't connect the dots looking forward; you can only connect them looking backwards. So you have to trust that the dots will somehow connect in your future. You have to trust in something—your gut, destiny, life, karma, whatever. This approach has never let me down, and it has made all the difference in my life." | Steve Jobs

In my career I always said I wanted to be in the healthcare business because I find it exciting. I didn't have a particular appetite for science when I was growing up; I had a hunger for math, but not biology, chemistry, or physics. I didn't really have much use for it then. I certainly do now, and while I ended up getting where I wanted to be, it was more a case of me saying, "I want to go into the business of healthcare and I want the top job in this space. I want to lead as many people as possible." So I always had that as a goal: leadership. But I was smart enough to realize if I was going to be successful, I better get as much experience as possible. Even if I had to take lateral steps along the way and do things that people would say didn't seem like advancements, I wanted *experience* so that when I got there, to the top, I wouldn't mess it up.

In the same way I didn't know what I was aiming for except experience to lead me to the top rank of leadership in the healthcare business, every step you've taken—both those taken intentionally and those unintentionally—will in the end wind up being 'on purpose.' There will be a reason why you've needed to learn what you did during the rough patches in your life, or in the less desirable jobs you've ever held, or the parts of life that just drove you absolutely insane when you were in them. Later on, you'll realize, "Ohhhh *yeah*, *that's* why I learned that... because I needed it for this." You'll connect the dots. But as Steve Jobs said, you can only connect the dots looking backwards.

Buckminster "Bucky" Fuller talks about a concept called precession. On page 142 of his book *Critical Path* he defines it by saying, scientifically speaking, "The Sun and the Earth are both bodies in motion. Despite the 180 degree gravitational pull of the in-motion Sun upon the in-motion Earth, precession makes Earth orbit around the Sun in a direction that is at ninety degrees—ie. at a right angle—to the direction of the Sun's gravitational pull." In *non*-scientific terms, he often told the story of the honey bee to explain. "Seemingly inadvertently, the honey bee goes about his business of gathering honey. At ninety degrees to his body and his flight path, his legs gather pollen from one flower and 'accidentally' take this pollen to the next flower, resulting in cross pollination. Precession is the action that occurs at ninety degrees to bodies in motion."[6]

So often people speak of passion and purpose interchangeably, almost as if they are the same thing. Utilizing Fuller's analogy, however, we begin to understand the difference between the two, yet see the synergistic connection they share and the correlation between them. If we ourselves are a body in motion, following our *passion*—just like the honey bee blissfully gathering nectar from one flower and then the next—then our *purpose* becomes more of an outcome a destination, a byproduct so to speak. Collecting honey is the bee's *passion*, but cross pollination becomes its *purpose*. The bee contributes enormously to life on earth, and we get pollination, the growth of crops, and the sustaining of life for humans and animals. The bee's purpose is at a ninety degree angle to its passion.

If you ask people, "Why are you here on this planet? What are you here to do? Who are you here to be?" Those are difficult questions to answer. But if you ask people what they're passionate about and what the goals are that inspire and fulfill them and what they really want to have achieved by the end of their life, they will be more likely to be able to answer those questions successfully. And if they simply pursue *that*—those passions and those goals and those achievements—by the end of their life, their purpose will have revealed itself. And then,

6   "About Fuller," Session 4 | The Buckminster Fuller Institute, January 1, 1970, https://www.bfi.org/about-fuller/resources/everything-i-know/session-4.

that difficult existential question, "Why are you here?" will, at long last, be able to be answered.

I chased a job for money once before. It was the worst thing I ever did, because I wasn't passionate about money. I was lured by the *idea* of it, which was short lived. That's one of the reasons passion is so important—it will help you ride out the tough times. If you're in something for the wrong reasons, it's hard to dig as deep as you need to in order to be truly successful—to be best in the world at that one thing only you can be best at. But if you're truly passionate about something, you can continue to pursue your goals even in the face of adversity, failure and rejection (think Thomas Edison, Colonel Sanders, and so many other of the world's greats who failed so very many times before they finally succeeded).

When I was finally released from the hospital, people would ask me, "Why are you going back to work so fast after what you just went through?" My answer was, "I love what I do." *I actually really and truly love what I do.* When I come into work every day, it's like a sport that I'm training for and competing in—that's the way I look at it. But this time—unlike in my college football days—my opponents aren't wearing helmets and pads, they're in suits. Or in the case of the villain we're *really* fighting, sepsis, we're up against an enemy that you don't really get to see or touch.

When you find out what your passion is and go after it, you end up wanting to wake up and go to work every day because you're excited about what you do.

I see it a lot with nurses and healthcare providers; you might say the job they do is their passion—it's their passion to care for people—but it also ultimately becomes, or is revealed to be, their purpose. As nurses, they're doing their technical "job." But in the case of my extra-mile nurse, I'm sure she felt as though her purpose was to be there beside me, giving me the support she could to help me make it through. That isn't a job, that's a calling. That is doing the bigger spiritual work within the context of the regular vocational work. Purpose and passion get inextricably linked and deeply intertwined.

There is a term within the healthcare field that is called "bedside manner." And there's a reputation amongst doctors and surgeons that suggests many people don't have a very good one. There is such an opportunity for healthcare professionals who are willing to go beyond their responsibility and be a human—to allow their humanity to show, like my extra-mile nurse did—in order to create a gap through which their purpose can reveal itself and bring greater meaning to the work they do day in, and day out. Staying closed off emotionally and "cold" to the patient is actually a disservice to both the patient *and* the practitioner, but especially the latter—sure you're saving lives, but I believe the feeling of meaning and purpose you experience and the richness of the reward is diminished if there is no connection to the life you've saved.

Several months ago I was at Mass General for my annual follow-up that involves a surgical procedure in the cath lab. Afterwards, I am required to lay on my back for four hours. Of course, I always bring my laptop so I can get some work done during those times. When I finally got tired of the laptop falling on my face (it's not easy to use a laptop laying on your back), I decided to just close my eyes and listen in to what was going on around me. I was outside of the cath lab, and the sound of the machines brought me back to the memory of being in the ICU—it was a very noisy place, with alarms going off regularly. As I was listening to the different noises I heard, the sound of some people's monitors gave me flashbacks. Before long I found myself listening to the voice of a patient—I could tell she was an elderly woman, and she was sort of nasty and demanding to the nurses. I couldn't help but think *Gosh, that nurse who is dealing with that woman is the most patient human being I have ever heard in my life.*

I didn't know how old she was, or what she looked like; I didn't know anything about her. I was just listening and thinking, *Wow, that's a real gift.* And, then I heard her voice again, interrupting my thoughts—only this time it was closer. She opened the curtain and came into my room, and now the same voice was right beside me. I whispered to her, "I'm blown away by the patience you showed with that patient. I would have responded *very* differently than you did." And she said, "That's why I do what I do."

That's why she does what she does. It's her calling. That's her genius. Her passion ultimately has become her purpose—to be a nurse, and to take care of people—making them feel better, and not just saving lives, but also saving souls through dignified respect and care and her full, patient attention and presence.

And I think my passion and purpose works exactly the same way.

When I left Chembio Diagnostics, a company with a healthy balance sheet and a bright future, to join a much smaller business, people would say, "What the heck would you do that for?"

Because it was in line with the experience I had just lived through.

During my time in the hospital, I learned an awful lot about the way antibiotics are prescribed for patients who are at risk of sepsis. And when I had to deal with multiple hospital-acquired infections that ultimately led to my own sepsis diagnosis, I was teetering on becoming one of those horrific, terrifying statistics.

I had heard about this company, T2 Biosystems, and I knew from being in the industry that T2 had the only technology that could detect these sepsis-causing pathogens directly from whole blood. And I also knew that the company had not done a terrific job on the commercialization of this technology. I'm what you would call a "commercially-slanted CEO"; I didn't grow up the way most CEOs grow up—through the financial side of the business—I grew up through the commercial side of big diagnostic companies. T2 had on the one hand, beautiful science, and on the other hand, poor execution. Great execution on the science, but poor execution in sales and marketing. I knew that I could lend my talents to this company and change the trajectory on the commercialization and try to solve this crisis, sepsis, that kills eleven million people worldwide each year.

Because T2 is a public company (NASDAQ: TTOO), I couldn't tell people in advance and ask them what they thought. So I did my own homework, determined as much of the risk as I could gain from being an outsider, and then I made the decision to pursue T2. I am so grateful that T2's first employee decided in 2009 to take the technology and gamble his first job away after his PhD to try to create something that would solve a problem that kills so many people each year. If he didn't do that, the company would not exist, and I wouldn't be here. His decision to create these groundbreaking products, combined with what I went through in my own medical journey and diagnosis, would actually allow me to pursue what is my TRUE PURPOSE—solving this sepsis issue once and for all, for all of us.

When the news came out, even though some of my friends and colleagues thought I was nuts to go to a company that they viewed as risky, I was excited and passionate about it and 100% committed.

Other people can't see your purpose because it's uniquely yours and yours alone. Only I could see that. And when I tried to explain it to them, I either couldn't, or I wasn't explaining it well enough for people to understand. So I ultimately decided to stop trying to explain it and decided to just *show* people instead. I told my friends to sit back and watch what we would do at this company under my leadership. I knew it would be totally different than anybody else had been able to do, or would ever be able to do. *I was created for this opportunity.* I went through everything I went through for this moment, even though I didn't know it at the time. I could use my gifts—these attributes that I was born with, or I developed over time: my ability to lead, my ability to communicate effectively with people, my intensity, my work ethic—I could apply all of them to this role. And I could pair it with my experience both as a patient and as a sepsis survivor and go on to solve a problem that causes the death of so many people that no one else has been able to figure out how to solve. And I could take all those things and use it as a platform to write this book, and speak, and change even more lives. And that's ultimately become my true purpose.

What happened didn't happen TO me, it happened FOR me.

And now it's my job to use that experience, and Alex's heart—along with my own H.E.A.R.T.—for good.

Thank you for the privilege of sharing the journey with me.

ACKNOWLEDGMENTS

I am the luckiest person on the planet; humbled and grateful beyond words. I'm blessed to have so many incredible people in my life to share this journey. I love you all more than words can express.

(THE COE FAMILY) PETER, PAM, EMILY: *I am so thankful for our relationship. Alex is forever a part of me and our families are inextricably linked. We are on this journey together.*

(MY SONS) JOHN, JEFF, and KYLE: *Being your father is the most precious gift in my lifetime. I am so honored to support and guide you to becoming the best possible versions of yourselves.*

(MY LOVE) RHONDA: *I am so grateful that life put us on this path together. You are truly my guardian angel and our relationship is one of the greatest blessings in my life.*

(MY MOM) PAT SPERZEL: *While you are no longer physically here, we are together in spirit every single day. Your love, support, attitude, and determination has made me who I am today.*

(MY DAD) JOHN SPERZEL: *I will always be proud to carry your namesake and do my best to honor and respect the things you instilled in me: integrity, hard work, excellence, and commitment.*

(MY SIBLINGS) BARBARA, JIM, and SUSAN: *Thank you for always being there, no matter what the circumstances, and for always having my back. I will always have yours.*

(MY OHANA) HOWARD and MARY HIGA: *I'm blessed to be part of such a great family. Thank you for creating the most amazing woman I have ever met, and my "sisters-in-law" Lisa and Shannon.*

MY COACHES & MENTORS: Dennis Macdonell, Norman Pessin, and Jay Cottone – *Thank you for pushing me to be better today than I was yesterday, and aiming even higher tomorrow.*

MY FRIENDS AND COLLEAGUES: *Whether old friends or new, near or far—I appreciate our time together and I am grateful for our friendship.*

MY INCREDIBLE BOOK TEAM: Krista Clive-Smith, Ashley Bunting, *and the* Merack Publishing team. *This book would not exist without your amazing talents. From the bottom of my heart, THANK YOU*

ABOUT
THE AUTHOR

John Sperzel is the President and Chief Executive Officer of T2 Biosystems, a leader in the rapid detection of sepsis-causing pathogens. His career in the healthcare diagnostics industry has spanned decades and has included work in the diabetes, critical care, and infectious disease sectors.

The Plymouth State University graduate and former college quarterback battled a rare condition that resulted in a heart transplant in 2017, which led to multiple hospital-acquired infections. John is passionate about stemming the tidal wave of sepsis-related deaths through T2 Biosystems' efforts to accelerate early detection and targeted treatments.

IN ONE YEAR, COVID KILLED
2.47 MILLION PEOPLE.

11 MILLION DIE OF SEPSIS EVERY YEAR.

AS ONE OF THE LUCKY SURVIVORS,
I'M ON A MISSION TO SOLVE THIS ISSUE
ONCE AND FOR ALL... FOR ALL OF US.

VISIT WWW.JOHNSPERZEL.COM/SEPSIS
TO JOIN THE MOVEMENT.

CPSIA information can be obtained
at www.ICGtesting.com
Printed in the USA
BVHW031211120421
604724BV00001B/24